On Edge

Mental Illness
in the Christian Context

Kristen Kansiewicz

The case examples in this book are based on real-life scenarios; however, all names and case details have been significantly altered to protect the privacy of any individuals upon which the story themes were based.

All websites or resources listed in this book were available at the time of this publication and may be subject to change. The resources are listed as suggestions but do not necessarily represent a full endorsement by the author.

This book is not intended to give or replace medical advice. The information provided should not be used for self-diagnosis. See a medical professional if you believe you are experiencing mental health symptoms.

Cover photo: Alex Emanuel Koch/Shutterstock
Cover design: Heather Cahill

ISBN: 1-501-01618-0
ISBN-13: 978-1-501-01618-9

To all those in the church who suffer from mental illness—may you encounter love and grace as we journey together as a body.

Contents

Acknowledgements

I have undertaken a huge challenge this year in writing a set of books to correspond with the Freedom Workshop Series. I could not have done this without the support of my husband, Joshua, and my children who have graciously given me time and space to write.

I also could not have done this without the support of my Lead Pastor, Kurt Lange, who gives me freedom to do what God has called me to do.

I would be hopelessly lost without East Coast International Church. This is a body of genuine and honest believers, for whom this book was written. Many of the stories within these pages are the stories of those who have overcome a tremendous amount in their lives and who have never pretended to be something they were not. Lynn is a city full of beautiful and resilient people, many of whom face significant mental illness challenges.

Thank you (again!) to my amazing editing team, particularly Laurie Hurshman who spent countless hours combing over every detail of this book. Thank you as well to the many people who contributed their stories to this book or gave permission to have their story written and shared. While details and names have been changed, these stories are real and have been offered graciously by those who seek to help others through sharing their experiences. Specifically, chapters 3, 7, 11, and 12 were written collaboratively with authors who chose to tell their stories anonymously.

And once again Heather Cahill has done an amazing job on the cover design for this book! I am so grateful for her willingness to go above and beyond to facilitate the process of readers (who of course DO judge books by their covers) actually opening the book.

Preface

Christians face very real physical and mental challenges every day. There has been a shifting conversation on the topic of mental health in the church in the past decade, and the goal of this book is to add to that conversation. It is my hope that Christians who have suffered and even questioned their faith because of their struggles with mental illness will find comfort and compassion within these pages. I also hope to educate those within the church on how to respond to others who are hurting.

There are four parts to this book. The first four chapters lay the foundation for understanding the debate within the church about mental health disorders, treatment options that Christians should consider, and the role of feelings in the faith journey. The second part of the book walks through some specific disorders, each illustrated by a case example based on real-life stories of Christians suffering from mental illness. These stories continue in part three as we examine other life crises and emotional problems that Christians face. We end with a final section addressing the role of the pastor in responding to mental health needs.

The case examples are based on real experiences, but I do not attempt to represent every person's experience in facing mental illness as a Christian. There are many ways that depression, for example, manifests in different people and in different life stages. Your own story is yours alone, and perhaps this book will inspire you to share it with others.

The church in America has come a long way in acknowledging the reality that mental illness is not the result of a person's own sin. We live in a cursed world where disorder abounds. God can and will heal all of us, some on this earth and some in eternity. The church also has a long way to go in ending stigma once and for all and becoming a safe place for all hurting people. I truly pray that this book will be a resource within the church to facilitate helpful and healing dialogue and to enable many to seek the treatment they need.

Part 1

Foundational Concepts: understanding Mental Illness in the Church

1

The Church and the Mental Health Revolution

Next time you are sitting in church, take a glance down your row. According to the National Alliance on Mental Illness (*www.nami.org*), one in four adults will experience mental illness in any given year. If the church is doing its job drawing in the hurting and broken, the percentage of adults within a church setting suffering from a mental illness should be *higher* than the general population.

If 25-33 percent of adults within the American church—and in some urban contexts a much higher percentage—are struggling with a mental illness within any given year, that means the church needs to be prepared to support and treat mental health needs. Some in the church already have treatment in place, though in many cases this treatment is with providers who do not share a Christian faith or worldview. For many Christians facing mental health issues, there is no history of prior treatment and when problems arise the first place they turn is the church.

That being said, the mental health revolution is a relatively new one, with words like "ego" and "self-esteem" being introduced only within the last century. Broader questions have certainly been asked since the beginning of modern history, as humans have sought to determine the nature of emotions. But it wasn't until the early 1900's that mental health as we now know it began to be studied in earnest.

In his book, *History of Psychology* (1984), David Hothersall outlines a comprehensive overview of the development of the field of psychology. He describes the Greek philosophers who first began to seek a connection between emotions and physical health. "Humors" were thought to be fluids in the body that affected mood.

Fast forward to the mid-1700's and new ideas (that turned out to be quite wrong) came along in a field called *phrenology*, in which scientists believed one's personality could be understood by feeling the shape of a person's skull. Despite their misguided efforts, the phrenologists were onto something—the brain is involved in mood and emotion regulation.

In the late-1800's, Wilhelm Wundt became the first to use a more modern scientific method to study observable measures of what was going on in the mind, such as documenting response times to a variety of stimuli. Others soon followed in studying memory, how we learn, and how and why we feel empathy.

As psychology became more established as a measurable science, some began to wonder about abnormal behavior. These were the earliest considerations of how we now define mental illness. Sigmund Freud famously studied "hysterical" women and also documented observations of child development. While there is certainly much of Freud's theory that has been rejected in the face of empiricism, culturally he played a major role in how we think about the "self."

Early behaviorism came along in 1910's and 1920's, with Ivan Pavlov and John Watson each demonstrating that a person could be "conditioned" into having a certain response. Pavlov, for example, rang a bell just before he was about to feed his dogs. After doing this enough times, he was able to demonstrate (by measuring the dogs' saliva) that the dogs had become conditioned to salivate upon hearing the bell, whether or not food was actually present.

By 1952, enough research had been done in the field of mental disorders that the American Psychiatric Association (established in 1921 and known as the APA) published its first Diagnostic and Statistical Manual, commonly known as the DSM. In a web article, "DSM: History of the Manual," the APA notes that in part the development of the DSM was a response by the military after World War II to provide clarity on documented mental problems seen in veterans (Web. www.psychiatry.org. Retrieved 6/9/14). By 1980, the DSM had been revised to include specific lists of criteria to help doctors and therapists assess patients with a variety of mental health symptoms.

Since the 1980's, medical and scientific advancements have dramatically changed our understanding of the brain and its role in emotions. As neuro-scientific understanding continues to expand, it is likely that we will see development of medical tests that can specifically measure complexities of brain functioning. At present, we continue to rely on observation of behavior to determine the presence of a mental disorder. This subjective process is certainly flawed, with both Christian and secular mental health clinicians cautioning against problems like over-diagnosing and over-prescribing of psychotropic medications.

Long before psychology came on the scene, the Bible offered insight into the emotional needs of all people. From this living word of God, we know we need relationship with God, we need a way out of sin, we need hope. But the Bible does not attempt to provide a how-to manual for treating specific mental illnesses, just as it does not attempt to describe how to treat broken bones or diabetes. These disorders, which scientists are only just beginning to understand, are specific physical problems that require qualified intervention.

The Christian response to the burgeoning field of psychology began with early Christian psychologists, including Clyde Narramore, who in 1958 established the Narramore Christian Foundation still in existence today. David Powlison chronicles the journey of Christian and biblical counseling in his book, *The Biblical Counseling Movement* (2010). He highlights the fact that pastors had been doing various forms of pastoral counseling for centuries, but a shift took place with Narramore and others who were Christians studying psychology but who were not pastors.

As these Christian psychiatrists and psychologists began to write and practice, their work primarily took place outside the walls of the church. They worked in secular environments and often worked with the general population, Christian or otherwise. Pastors, and in particular a pastor named Jay Adams, began to take issue with the idea that psychological theories and methods were being offered as a response to problems that had once been handled within the church setting by pastors.

In the mid-1960's, seminaries and Christian colleges began to offer psychology and Christian counseling degrees. These programs emphasized (and still maintain) an integration between the study of psychology and the Bible. Beginning from a Christian view of the human person, this integrative approach incorporates modern study of the brain and various psychological techniques with the Bible and theology.

Jay Adams, founder of "biblical counseling," spoke out strongly against the study of psychology and psychiatry. He asserted that sin is the fundamental root issue of problems unless there is a specific "organic disorder" (a physical problem detected by a direct medical test, such as a blood test). He did not agree with the way in which psychiatrists diagnosed mental illnesses using only subjective measures before prescribing medications. Adams believed that the Bible had provided every answer needed for a range of emotional problems, and the biblical counseling approach seeks to only offer advice or counsel that comes directly from Scripture.

This debate within the church—biblical counseling versus an integrative Christian counseling—has led to a strong divide that persists today. Efforts have been made to bring the two sides together to find common ground, but historically such attempts have accomplished little. Within the past decade, organizations like the the Christian Counseling and Educational Foundation (known as CCEF and originally founded by Adams in 1968) have sought to bring together ideas that Christians can study and use psychology *and* that these Christian counselors also need a strong biblical and theological foundation both in theory and in practice.

Average church attendees, who are likely unaware of this historical debate within the church about how to respond to mental illness and emotional problems, may find themselves caught in the crosshairs. In his book *Grace for the Afflicted*, Matthew Stanford shares his surprise and dismay in encountering Christians who did not believe mental illness—in this case depression—could happen to "true" Christians (2008. Madison, WI: InterVarsity Press. pp. 73-

74). In the American church culture, many have been taught that emotional problems are only a spiritual issue. It is only recently that the physical and clinical aspects of mental illness have been openly discussed in churches across America.

Pastors across many denominations and in non-denominational churches are likely to have an opinion on how to best provide counseling to their parishioners, and these opinions may be very different. Most pastors handle common, everyday struggles by offering pastoral counseling, and this is usually the first step when a church member is looking for help. What happens next may vary widely—some pastors will continue to counsel the person using a biblical counseling approach (sometimes called *nouthetic counseling*) and others will refer the person to an outside Christian counseling practice that will most likely bill your medical insurance and will use some type of integrative approach. Some pastors may encourage people to take medications if needed, while others may strongly disagree with most use of medications for emotional problems.

The Church Therapy model is a newer approach that brings together elements from both sides of the church-mental health debate. In this model, a professionally trained, licensed

Christian counselor works on a church staff alongside and in conjunction with the pastors. The counselor in this context provides professional Christian counseling to those in the church who are facing more severe mental health issues or abuse histories. This model increases accessibility to quality care and decreases the stigma of going to counseling, as mental health becomes an integral part of the internal church culture and dialogue. (For more on the Church Therapy model, take a look at my blog: *www.churchtherapy.com*).

Across the country, more and more pastors are beginning to speak out about mental health problems among Christians to raise awareness of an often hidden problem. Radio programs such as New Life Ministries and Focus on the Family have been critical to the conversation in the last twenty years. More recently, Rick Warren hosted a conference on mental health issues, marking the one-year anniversary of his son's death by suicide.

The remainder of this book seeks to engage in this conversation as we look at specific disorders, emotional challenges, and the role of the pastor in addressing mental health issues. How we choose to handle the delicate problems presented in our churches matters. It matters because every day many Christians continue to struggle with problems like depression, anxiety, trauma, and mania. It matters because an inadequate or untrained response harms people. It matters because in some churches people feel they must silently suffer, or seek mental health treatment in a way that their pastor has discouraged.

This book seeks to respond in a Christian manner from a professionally trained perspective to a variety of tough questions. Please note the use of the word "respond" as opposed to "answer"—the questions that are posed in these chapters have no easy answers. You will not walk away from reading this book with a neatly tied-up position on mental health in the Christian life. Almost all of these questions have been posed to me in my work as a church therapist by people who have been caught in the middle of the debate described earlier. Many continue to struggle with the reality of their lives as they battle mental illness and seek to follow Jesus every day. Any response to their struggle can only hope to be loving, careful, and founded upon the highest level of biblical and scientific study.

2

Is Mental Illness Real?

Christians live in a strange, in-between place. We know that Jesus conquered sin and death on the cross, and His work is done; His kingdom has come and yet is still coming. We live in a sin-cursed world, yet we know it is not our home. We know we are free from sin, yet we remain sinners each and every day. We know healing is possible, yet we continue to suffer from disease.

Our brains are just as prone to illness as the rest of our bodies are. When our brains are disrupted, whether chemically or structurally, illness manifests in a variety of ways. Emotions, heavily regulated by the limbic system in the brain, can become dysregulated. Excessively negative thinking, obsessions, highly anxious thoughts or feelings, hallucinations, and delusions are all examples of brain dysregulation. Considering mental illness becomes complicated as some Christians may try to fit these symptoms into their theology of self-control, joy, peace, or trusting in God. While there are certainly spiritual problems that can cause someone to feel depressed for a while, true clinical depression and other diagnosable mental illnesses are physical in nature.

Some Christians may argue this point, perhaps suggesting that symptoms of depression, for example, are too subjective to measure. If you can't take a blood test or a brain scan and find an abnormality, you don't have a true illness. While it would be wonderful to have a concrete medical test for depression or other mental illnesses, the absence of a medical test does not necessarily mean an absence of disease. For example, specific diabetes symptoms were noted for at least 300 years before a medical test was developed to easily detect its presence. Similarly, breast cancer existed long before the development of the mammogram in the 1950s.

Medical science can take decades, if not centuries, to develop objective, measurable tests that pinpoint the presence of a specific disease. It is not unusual for subjective symptoms to be noted and researched first, as this early stage of disease detection is necessary to even begin the process of developing specific laboratory tests.

The more complex the organ function, the more difficult it will likely be to develop a valid and reliable medical test.

The brain is the most complex organ in the body. While we often compare it to the central processing unit of a computer, the brain is far more intricate than a programmed device. It is capable of adaptation and change. Only in the past 50 years have we begun to scratch the surface of brain dysfunction, and only in the past decade or so have we developed tests for early Alzheimer's detection. We have a long way to go in the field of neuroscience.

So what does all this science talk have to do with a Christian worldview? Isn't that just secular theory? Won't faith in God bring Christians through anything they are going through? Medical science is extremely important for the Christian life as we seek to care for our bodies. If there were a simple blood test that could measure brain functioning, or a scan that could detect depression in the brain, the Christian struggling with mental illness would just go to her doctor, get a test, and take medication for a physical condition. She probably wouldn't give it any more thought than if she had high cholesterol.

However, because we have not yet developed objective measures, doctors and counselors are currently forced to rely on their observations of mood and behavior. The patient comes in, explains what he or she has been feeling, and the doctor must decide from this self-report how best to treat the depressed patient. With this current method, medications can tend to be over-prescribed as primary care doctors are hurried and have less expertise in mental health disorders.

With these flaws in the proper diagnosis of mental health disorders such as depression or anxiety, some Christians dismiss mental illness altogether. When you are struggling with symptoms of mental illness, you may feel like it is just "all in your head." This way of thinking leads the church down a road of blaming those that are truly ill for their illnesses.

Because of that in-between place of embracing the kingdom of God while we wait for it to be fully realized with Christ's return, we fall victim to disease just like the rest of humanity. Satan is still actively at work in the world, and all types of illnesses are some of the fruit of his labors. Some who suffer from depression or other mental illnesses may find themselves blaming God, but in reality it is Satan who is to blame for our suffering in this broken world. In the midst of this reality, the church needs to be a place where the broken and hurting feel safe.

The church must be a place where hope resides, where love endures, and where emotional safety flourishes, for it is Christ alone who offers a way out of our present suffering. Christ alone will walk alongside us as One who has also suffered.

Emotions are complicated. Those who do not struggle with mental diseases or dysfunction often have difficulty understanding the plight of those who do suffer. If you are seemingly able to control your emotions, why shouldn't all other Christians be able to do the same? If someone in your church can't control her emotions or do something to fix them, what does this mean about the Holy Spirit in her life? If emotions are off-balance, doesn't that mean that one's spiritual life is off-balance as well?

If a Christian had breast cancer, would this diagnosis mean the Holy Spirit had left her? Would the development of diabetes mean that this faithful Christian had stopped trusting in God? If another had a stroke and was immobilized, if his speech became disrupted as a result, would these be a result of his own sin? Of course not. Neither is mental illness a result of one's own personal sin.

Treatment of mental illnesses requires a well-rounded approach, including therapy and sometimes medication. The need for medication will depend on the severity of symptoms as well as how well therapy and coping strategies work to bring the illness under control. The causes of mental illness can be varied and complicated. Addressing the underlying causes through a combination of medication and counseling has been shown to be the most effective treatment for these symptoms.

3

Should Christians Take Psychiatric Medications?

Let's transition now from the more abstract to the practical, looking to real stories of real Christians to help illustrate the question of each of the remaining chapters. We will look at specific case examples, often written by or co-written with anonymous authors willing to share their stories. Their stories will be followed by a response from a Christian counseling perspective, exploring psychological principles and scientific research from a biblical foundation. Medication is a topic of great debate and personal concern for many Christians seeking to treat mental health symptoms. Catherine, our case example for this chapter, shares her personal journey as we consider how to approach psychiatric medications from a Christian worldview.

Case Example

Catherine had struggled with anxiety for a long time. She wasn't sure what tipped her into depression, but it seemed like a combination of causes: she had been in a five-year relationship that she thought would lead to marriage, but instead it ended. One and a half years later, she hadn't met anyone else, and her hopes for getting married in the future were dwindling. Work was also very stressful and felt out of control. Catherine's sense of worth and being able to handle things started to shoot down.

Catherine began to use eating and food as a way to feel in control again. Without even realizing it, she began to develop an eating disorder as she carefully calculated what she would eat. Catherine felt like she was accomplishing something when she ate less and less and convinced herself that she didn't need food. Within a few months, she had become very self-focused. Catherine felt restless, slept little, and generally felt "sick"—like she had a "flu" of sadness, anxiety, hopelessness, and a loss of joy. She remembers thinking that maybe it wouldn't be so bad if she died. Crossing the street became an opportunity to see if maybe a car would hit her and she wouldn't have to struggle like this anymore.

Catherine had no idea she was dealing with depression, because she had never had a depressive episode before. Her friends and family knew her as a very happy, friendly person—that's how she had been all her life. Now they (and she) saw someone completely different. People expressed worry and concern about her.

Catherine was already in therapy with a professional Christian counselor. Her counselor brought up the possibility of talking to her doctor about trying an anti-depressant. "Me?" Catherine thought. "I shouldn't have to go on medication for depression. Other people do that, but not me." She wasn't ready to seriously consider it.

But as a few months passed, Catherine's depression felt worse and deeper. She was also losing a lot of weight. She agreed to make an appointment with her doctor, who expressed concern. Catherine's doctor told her that she prescribed anti-depressants for a lot of her patients, who need them for a time, and can then go off the medication. As her doctor normalized the idea a bit, it took away some of the shame for Catherine, the feeling that "I shouldn't need medication for this." Catherine's doctor also told her that she might not need to take the medication forever. If she decided to take it, her doctor would start her off on a small dosage, and monitor her to see whether the dose needed to be increased. If it didn't work, she could try a different medication. If it did work, Catherine would start to feel more like herself again. Her doctor told Catherine that this wasn't a "happy pill," but that if it worked for her, she might smile or laugh a little more. She'd feel more like herself again.

Catherine's doctor gave her the prescription, and Catherine held onto it for awhile. Catherine still wasn't ready to try this route. She thought maybe she could get better without it. Besides, maybe she was supposed to struggle through this "depressive episode," and God would bring her out of it when He was ready. Medicating herself for depression seemed like a thing that privileged, over-worked, over-stressed Westerners did. If she just depended more on God, He'd bring her out of this when He was ready to. Catherine didn't need to "fix it" with a pill. That seemed like the easy way out.

Catherine's mother also told her that she worried that if Catherine started taking medication, it might make her feel better, and then she'd never do the work of figuring out the underlying causes that led to her depression in the first place. Her mother also worried about when Catherine would stop taking the meds; she'd heard stories about people becoming suicidal if they stopped taking anti-depressants too quickly. (Catherine didn't want to scare her mother, so she didn't tell her that she was already having semi-suicidal thoughts!)

Catherine's counselor encouraged her by telling her that she would most likely be starting on a very small dose. She told Catherine that she probably wouldn't feel any different until her doctor gradually increased the dosage. So Catherine started taking Celexa. Her doctor gradually increased the dosage. She had to increase it very slowly, as at first Catherine felt a little dizzy and lightheaded from taking the pill. It also made her feel more awake when she took it at night, as her doctor had recommended, so instead she started taking it in the morning. Catherine didn't feel any different for the first two or three months of taking the medication.

Catherine remembers the day when she realized she was feeling more like herself again. She was standing in front of her bathroom mirror, putting on makeup and thinking about the day ahead. Her friends were getting together. For the past few months she had been avoiding them, just wanting to isolate herself and be alone. Catherine had had no social energy. But now, she realized that she actually wanted to be with her girlfriends that night. That felt more like the person she was before depression.

From then on, Catherine's symptoms did not totally go away. But she felt thankful that she had started taking Celexa, because whatever it did in her brain enabled her to function at a level at which she had been unable in her depressed state. She had more energy and mental clarity to deal with her sense of hopelessness about the future, and the way she was striving for perfection at work. With the encouragement of her counselor and her family, Catherine found a very kind nutritionist who was very familiar with eating disorders. With the nutritionist, Catherine developed a healthier eating plan, and she helped Catherine to realize why she was striving for "thin-ness." It really was about control and a sense of wanting to achieve something...but in the process, Catherine was destroying her body. With the nutritionist's help and a lot of prayer from her family and friends, Catherine gradually started to gain back the weight she had lost, and also started forming healthier attitudes about food and exercise.

In the following months, as Catherine continued taking Celexa, going to therapy, and seeing her nutritionist, she started to get better.

A little less than one year after she started taking the medication, Catherine's doctor and counselor thought she was ready to start tapering off. At first she did so too quickly, and randomly had very dark thoughts run through her mind, ones that reminded her of when she was depressed. She called her doctor, who helped develop a very slow tapering-off plan, because Catherine's body was proving to be very sensitive to the change in dosage. Over many months, she gradually tapered off the Celexa, and eventually stopped taking it altogether.

Catherine is really thankful for the encouragement of her therapist and doctor to start taking an antidepressant. Would God have brought her out of depression if she hadn't taken the medication? Maybe. But it also scares her to think of what she could have done to herself if she had stayed in that depression for much longer. She was already starving herself, and her body was suffering. She still feels guilty sometimes for "giving in" and taking an antidepressant. But she does think that God used it to help her heal, and she's really grateful for that. In the future, if she starts developing signs of depression again, Catherine thinks she would be open to taking the medication again.

Counselor's Response

Catherine's story is similar the experiences of many in the church. For a variety of reasons, symptoms of mental illness become present and require treatment, including medication in some cases. For many who have not had mental health treatment before, the idea of taking medication for emotional symptoms seems foreign, scary, or even morally wrong.

Medication is not necessary in all cases. For many, simply talking about their problems and developing new coping skills and new ways of thinking is enough. For many others, these strategies help a little, but the physical and mental symptoms are too intense or persist for too long to go away without medical intervention.

Before you take any medication, you should talk with your doctor about your options. Catherine found that Celexa worked well for her, others may find that another medication targets their symptoms better. Your doctor or psychiatrist can help you determine what medication may be right for you, and they can evaluate whether or not you truly need medication. A professional Christian counselor is often a good first step, as he or she will be able to help you with coping and other strategies to try before deciding to ask your doctor about medication. Unless you are having thoughts of hurting yourself or someone else or are hearing or seeing things that others do not, you may want to try things like exercise, writing in a journal, or muscle relaxation first. If these behavioral strategies do not work effectively to reduce your symptoms, medication may be necessary.

Many people have asked, "Isn't taking medication just the easy way out?" Some fear that taking medication is an excuse not to work through their problems, or they view it as an admission that they do not trust God. These views of medication give it a much higher power than it actually has. Medication will not take away your problems. It is not in opposition to God, and many have to trust God more in the process of trying medication that they feel nervous about taking. No medication will take away all of your symptoms, and you should not feel "drugged" or "out of it" when your symptoms are properly treated.

Medication is simply a tool. It is one piece of the treatment puzzle that actually works best when combined with counseling, as numerous studies have shown. When your emotional symptoms are treated, you are able to think and feel more like yourself again. You will continue to have problems, but you will likely find that you have more energy to actually face them and make some changes in your life. You may find that you are able to enjoy life again, and this may actually help you to relate to God better.

As with any medication for any illness, there is the potential for side effects or reactions. Not every medication works for everyone, and unfortunately sometimes there is a trial-and-error process in finding the right one for you. As medical advances progress, perhaps we will develop more accurate ways to test for specific mental illnesses and be able to know in advance which medications will work best to target each specific brain dysfunction. For now, hang in there. Medication is not the answer to all of your issues, but it is worth trying when you and your doctor feel that the risk of not treating your symptoms outweighs the risks of taking medication.

Untreated symptoms of anxiety, depression, or other disorders can be fatal (see chapter 14 for a discussion on suicide). Some studies have also found links between untreated depression and other diseases such as heart disease, diabetes, Alzheimer's. If you feel that your symptoms are getting worse or are not helped by some simple lifestyle changes (such as diet and exercise), you may be putting other aspects of your health at risk.

Jesus came to earth as a healer, and when we take steps towards health we are participating in the restoration of our bodies. In our modern era and society, some of the tools that bring about healing are medicine, surgery, and physical therapies. As Christians, we trust and believe in God for healing, not by rejecting the medical treatments available to us, but by recognizing that it is always God's power at work that brings healing. He can and does heal in miraculous ways and through modern medical technologies. We do not make medicine our god, but we thankfully receive all that God has given us to promote life and wellness. Whether we suffer from diabetes, cancer, depression, or schizophrenia, we can experience recovery and wholeness by seeking God and seeking any treatment available to us.

4

Is Faith a Feeling?

As we conclude Part 1, we will consider the role of feelings as they relate to our understanding of God and faith. Even for those who do not struggle with mental illness, feelings and moods can have significant positive and negative impacts on the spiritual life. For those who do have a mental illness, faith and emotions can become a complicated mix. Let's turn to Dave, in our case example, to help us grapple with these ideas in real-life circumstances.

Case Example

Throughout his adolescence and adult life, Dave had been impulsive. Sometimes this ability to take quick action worked to his advantage, as he trusted God to carry him through. At other times, it was pure hot-temperedness—if he had not encountered people to talk him out of his plans to get even, who knows what might have happened? For all of this anger, there were other moments in which Dave was almost too forgiving. In the heat of the moment, he ultimately backed down.

When questioned by others, Dave chalked up a lot of his decisions to his faith and trust in God. It seemed irrational, sometimes downright stupid even to other believers around him. Yet his willingness to follow his gut and listen to God was often confirmed by a seemingly miraculous outcome. Not many people Dave knew had walked with God in this way.

Sin crept into Dave's life at times because his feelings could lead him astray. It seemed as though when he got an idea in his head he was going to take action without pausing to think about the consequences. A married man, Dave ended up having a one-night stand that resulted in a child. Using sin to cover his previous sin, Dave lied to avoid getting caught. Dave felt so horrible for all he had done that he shut himself up for a week, crying and unable to eat.

Sometimes Dave just needed to process and clear his head when his feelings became overwhelming. As a writer and musician, he could just lose himself in his music and it felt good. He connected with God strongly in these moments. Through the "highs" he danced and jumped for joy, and in his darker moments he cried out in utter confusion to God. In song Dave wrestled with his own struggles with anger, and while it was hard in the moment he sang about taking time to think instead of letting anger take over.

Feelings sometimes seemed to define Dave's life. He loved deeply, he mourned deeply, and he trusted God deeply. Feelings helped him encounter God and when the Spirit spoke to him it was an emotional experience. Through his own feelings, Dave could relate to God's feelings which helped to put things in perspective and give Dave a healthy fear of God. Sometimes he bargained with God, begging Him to do something about the problems he faced. When his son died tragically, Dave was so overcome with emotion that he wondered how he could even go on.

Just before his own death, Dave reflected on his life and wrote a song to capture his feelings. In the end he felt that God had spoken through him and had worked throughout his life to lead him. Dave hadn't been perfect, but his emotional experience of life and God had driven him in leadership. Perhaps because he never shied away from feeling, he had developed a deep intimacy with God and was confident to the end that God was on his side. He deeply loved God and felt God's love for him.

Passion. Intensity. Heartache. Victory. All of these emotional experiences defined Dave's life both spiritually and in his other relationships. To strip him of his emotional way of dealing with the world would have changed his very nature. His faith was strengthened because of his feelings of hope. His love for God endured because his feelings carried him through and helped him acknowledge the hand of God directly leading his life. Dave was a man who was not afraid to wear his heart on his sleeve, with no sense that a "real man" should be emotionless.

Counselor's Response

Many of you have probably figured out that the man in our story is actually King David from the Bible. You can read about his life in 1 and 2 Samuel and you can get a sense of his deep emotional life reading the book of Psalms. "Dave," like many of us, related to God through his emotions.

Our American culture often places a heavy emphasis on doing whatever "feels right," and as a result American Christians have responded by noting the dangers of feelings. A simple Google search for "feelings in the Bible" results in links to lists of Bible verses that point out the dangers of listening to your feelings. At the same time, we often talk about the fruit of the Holy Spirit as if it were a list of feelings: love, joy, peace—aren't those feelings? Are we supposed to get rid of our emotions in order to focus on truth, or are we supposed to replace our bad feelings with better feelings in order to spiritually grow?

As illustrated in the story opening this chapter, one's emotional life can be deeply useful in relating to God. Even Jesus Himself chose to become human and experienced a broad range of emotions, including deep sadness and anger as well as contentedness and love. There is something inherently human in the raw vulnerability of emotions—they help us engage with the world around us.

However, it is true that sometimes our feelings cannot be trusted. In the case of a mental illness, sometimes our emotions do not even accurately reflect our true selves, instead presenting a distorted version of our intended emotional state. We must cling to truth to provide stability through all of our emotional states, while at the same time not rejecting our feelings, as they can help us understand and relate to God and each other.

Throughout this book, we will journey through the impact of mental dysfunction on our spiritual lives. Before we explore those topics, it is important to establish that feelings are an important part of the way we process our lives and our relationship with God. In opening ourselves emotionally to God, we allow Him to work in the deepest places in our hearts to heal brokenness and pain and to fill us with His love.

Equally important to note is that feelings cannot define truth. God alone can define reality, and His word creates truth. All humans must humbly acknowledge their inability to feel and perceive truth accurately. We must use all of our senses, including but not limited to our feelings, in order to relate to God and understand His word.

As previously mentioned, the fruit of the Spirit (listed in Galatians 5) is often taken as a list of feelings. For someone with depression, for example, what does joy look like? In the case of anxiety, where is peace? The evidence of the Holy Spirit is certainly far greater than an emotional state—feelings come and go, but the Holy Spirit's work in our lives does not. God can and does work in the lives of the depressed, anxious, schizophrenic, bipolar, and grief-stricken. The peace that defies all sensibilities is powerful enough to exist even in an emotional atmosphere that is broken, wounded, and hurting. Since faith, hope, and love will endure forever (1 Cor. 13:13), surely One far greater than ourselves will carry these realities for us when we are in too much pain to feel it. It is *because* of the power of the Holy Spirit that we can trust His work in our lives even when our feelings suggest otherwise. God has chosen to work not in the healthy, but in the sick, to demonstrate His power.

Emotions are a tool for us that can enable us to experience life and God. Beauty, interconnection, and a sense of need for a Savior are all understood through emotional senses. But this tool does not provide a definition of reality—God alone can set reality in motion. Feelings must always remain in proper alignment to the One who sets truth in order. When we find that any of our senses lead us astray, we must cling to the truth of the God who is greater than all things.

Part 2

Specific Mental Health Disorders

5

Why Is God So Close and Yet So Far? The Bipolar Experience

Case Example

Pete was totally on fire for God. He loved going to church, studying the Bible, and listening to Christian music. Sometimes he prayed for hours, even sometimes praying all the way through the night. When Pete walked down the street, he said a hearty "Hello!" to each passerby and frequently told strangers about his faith in Jesus. Pete was involved in five different ministries in his church and seemed to have endless energy for serving others.

Some people in the church admired Pete's enthusiasm and relentless spirit. It seemed that Pete was on a constant spiritual mountaintop, and some envied Pete's spiritual life. "He must be so spiritually strong," they thought. From a distance, Pete seemed like a super-Christian.

In Pete's heart, he truly believed that he was closer to God than most other Christians. He regularly thought of himself as having an inside-line to God. Pete found connections in everything—seeing God in things others did not seem to notice. Often when Pete read the Bible, he found meaning in the words that others did not seem to understand. When he shared his observations at church, some others suggested he might not be accurate in his understanding of the Bible's meaning. Pete did not see how they could think his ideas were wrong. After all, he spent hours in prayer every day. He doubted that the others did so as faithfully.

Pete's pastor had some concerns about Pete's behavior. Despite the fact that he freely and frequently shared his faith, Pete sometimes did not show much depth in the application of the Bible to his own life. He could out-preach any street preacher, but Pete's pastor knew that he struggled with sleeping around and that his financial life was a mess. He appreciated Pete's willingness and energy, but something didn't seem quite right.

After a few months, Pete stopped coming to church. Many in the church reached out to him, but he didn't seem to be returning any of their calls. After a while, most people in the church kind of moved on and didn't really think much about Pete. His pastor decided to stop by Pete's apartment one day, and was quite surprised to see Pete looking disheveled and depressed. "Are you okay?" the pastor asked, bewildered. This was not the Pete he had known for the last year.

Pete shared with his pastor that he had not been doing well. "I can't even pray anymore, I feel like God doesn't answer me. He's just gone. I felt so close to God before, like He was filling me up and I could hear Him speaking to me. Now I hear absolutely nothing. I'm not sure I even believe in God now." Pete's pastor encouraged him to trust that God had not changed, and continue to pray even if he felt God wasn't listening. But when he went home that night, Pete's pastor wondered, "How could Pete have been on such a spiritual mountaintop and yet sink into a valley so quickly?"

Counselor's Response

As we have already discussed in chapter 4, feelings are not an accurate measure of faith. All of us have periods of time when we feel very close to God—mountaintop moments or spiritual highs. And we all have dark points as well, when God seems distant and it is a struggle to keep the faith. If our feelings were a good gauge of spiritual reality, then God would come and go in unpredictable patterns. Yet we know from the Bible that God is faithful and unchanging. He is there when we feel Him and there when we do not.

Some Christians face an extreme version of these ups and downs, and theirs is a real and physical struggle with Bipolar Disorder. Pete, described earlier, was in a manic phase when he started going to his church. His endless energy seemed like a good thing, and it even made him seem like a "superior" Christian. After all, he was praying all the time, preaching the Gospel, and serving others tirelessly. Despite these outward actions, Pete's inward spiritual life did not seem to line up. His pastor had noticed that he seemed spiritually strong and spiritually weak all at the same time. Those in the church who did not know Pete admired him and assumed that he was very spiritually mature.

The problem with using feelings to assess one's spiritual maturity is that feelings change. What goes up must come down—true for gravity and true for mania. These spiritual and emotional highs cannot last, and a crash of depression often creates a startling shift in one's relationship with God.

The end of a manic episode is a difficult loss in and of itself. Being extremely creative, energetic, and passionate is a fun ride. But when this high has also been associated with extreme closeness to God, the crash and the loss are devastating. There is a loss of one's self and a second loss of one's spiritual understanding.

So what does it mean to be a Christian with Bipolar Disorder? How can you find stability in your spiritual life when your feelings are so up and down? Because your feelings are not a good gauge of reality, spiritual or otherwise, you need systems in your life that help keep you grounded. These stabilizing forces can help keep you on track both in mania and in depression. The hardest part is forcing yourself to keep these systems in place at your highest high or your lowest low. When you are on a high, you will be convinced you do not need grounding. When you are in a low valley, you will wonder why you should even bother to try.

The first grounding system you need is feedback from others. Finding a safe counselor, mentor, pastor, or friend who can reflect back what they are seeing in your behavior and attitudes is critical to your self-awareness. In Romans 12:3 the Bible tells us to think of ourselves with "sober judgment," but when you have Bipolar Disorder this is nearly impossible to do by yourself. Choosing to place the opinions of safe supports over your own view of reality can help ground you.

Another way to keep yourself grounded is to focus on truth. Feelings change, truth stays the same. To remind yourself of this, every day regardless of your mood take a moment at the start of your day and drop your Bible onto the floor (the printed copy is not sacred—just the words inside!). As you do this, remind yourself that gravity is one example of a truth that stays the same no matter how you feel. Then pick your Bible up and read it, using a study guide or devotional to focus your thinking on truth rather than on looking for your own connections.

One final strategy for keeping yourself grounded is to develop routines of obedience to God. His desires for your life do not change with your moods. What is it that you can do to follow God on both your lowest day and your highest one? What consistency or common thread can your life hold that ties all of your spiritual life together? Choose a theme for the year that can remain constant no matter how you feel. What does God want to do in your life this year? In each day, keep this larger goal in mind as you develop routines that keep your life in line with God's work in your life.

In this struggle, it is critical to get professional help, often including medication, to regulate mood symptoms. Manic episodes can seem fun, but they can sometimes be dangerous. For those with Bipolar Disorder, taking medication is an intentional commitment to make. When you are manic, you may feel as though medication dulls your senses or changes your personality. When you are depressed, you may not care about your life enough to reach out for help. For some who do take medication for a while, it is easy to decide to stop taking them when you feel better for a while. Developing consistency and discipline in treatment can be a good starting point for putting such habits into practice in other areas of life.

6

Can Real Christians Be Depressed?

Case Example

Vanessa was a 46-year-old mother of four who had been active in her church for over ten years. She was known by others for her cheerful smile, and many said that Jesus just shined right through her. For many years, Vanessa felt happy most of the time and was genuine in her love for God and for others.

When Vanessa hit her 40s, she felt blindsided by life transitions. Her kids were growing up and getting ready to leave home, she started to lose interest in spending time with friends, and she struggled to have any kind of passion for ministry. At church, she tried to put on a smiling face, but inside she felt like a completely different person than she had ever known before.

It took several years for Vanessa to figure out what was going on in her heart and mind. At first, her long-time mentor suggested that maybe she was having some kind of spiritual crisis. Maybe Vanessa just wasn't trusting God to help her navigate these life transitions. Vanessa's pastor gave her some encouraging verses from the Bible and prayed with her, which did help her thinking some of the time, but on her dark days it seemed impossible to focus on anything positive.

Vanessa's relationships began to crumble around her as she pulled away from her friends and her husband. "You just aren't yourself anymore," her husband said one day. That statement stuck in Vanessa's mind as she looked back on her life to this point. Her faith in God had not changed, her goals to serve God and others had not changed, and yet it felt as though her mind and body had been taken over by something else. She had asked for prayer many times, but her struggles remained.

One night while watching TV Vanessa saw a commercial that described her to a tee. A little cartoon figure was walking along, a dark cloud following overhead. "Sometimes you don't feel like yourself," the announcer declared. "If you have experienced sadness, feelings of worthlessness, weight loss or gain, sleep problems, have had trouble getting out of bed or getting through the day, or if you have even had thoughts of suicide for at least two weeks, you may be suffering from depression. Talk to your doctor about your symptoms to see if an antidepressant may be right for you."

Vanessa clicked off the television and sat in a daze. Depressed? She had never considered herself to be a depressed person. But the description could not have been more spot on. Two weeks... more like two years by now. "But I can't be depressed," she thought. "I'm a Christian, I have hope in God, the Holy Spirit is supposed to fill me with joy..." But Vanessa just couldn't shake the question: can Christians be depressed?

Counselor's Response

"Depressed" is a word often used in our vocabulary to describe someone who is sad or feeling down. Casually we think of being depressed as simply a negative mood. Some have suggested that a life of sin apart from Christ is in itself a depressing existence. But for the Christian who is trusting in God with faith, depression can still become a very real problem.

And it is not a problem anyone would intentionally bring upon himself, nor would anyone choose to continue to live in a depressed state if he knew of a way out.

Clinical depression is not just a bad mood or a negative outlook on life. According to the DSM-5, it is characterized by at least two weeks of consistent symptoms, including disrupted sleep or eating, feelings of hopelessness or worthlessness, restlessness, a sense of detachment from one's own life, and even suicidal thoughts or wishes for death. Depressed mood is another symptom, but it is only one sign that must be accompanied by at least several of the others listed.

Widely cited research by NAMI and other groups suggest that about 25% of Americans will experience depression at some point in their adult lives. For some, a sudden stressor or a change in life circumstances can create a physical onset of depression. Others may not be able to connect its onset to a specific starting point. For some women, pregnancy and postpartum hormonal changes create an onset of lingering depression during what they had hoped would be the most exciting time of life. And of course there are some for whom depression begins in childhood or adolescence, and these sufferers face a more chronic and cyclical form of the illness.

Treatment for depression can include counseling and sometimes medication. Because of some of the very physical manifestations of depression—particularly insomnia or weight loss or gain—some may seek medical help for these symptoms prior to fully understanding the nature of depression or the connection between their physical symptoms and their overall mental health. As was the case for Vanessa, a diagnosis of depression may not come quickly as the person may focus on the stress in his or her life.

When true clinical depression has taken over in the brain, removal of one's life stress does not remove the depression symptoms. Even those things that led to the onset of depression do not need to remain for the depression to continue. Reducing your stress is important, but if you continue to have difficulty sleeping, are still losing or gaining weight, or you maintain the feelings of hopelessness or sadness even when you think you "should" feel better, then it is likely you need a combination of counseling and medication to reduce your symptoms. For those who do not have chronic depression, medication can stabilize you for a period of time and then be discontinued with your doctor's oversight. Your symptoms may have resolved and the episode of depression ends.

For some, episodes of depression come and go over a period of years or decades. Others do not experience depression in episodes, but rather have a low-level depression that does not lift for several years or more at a time. Meeting with a Christian counselor as well as with your doctor can help as you seek to understand your symptoms and get help.

There are many non-medication strategies that can help alleviate depression as well. Exercise is perhaps the most effective, although it can be hard to find the motivation to do so when you are depressed. A professional Christian counselor can work with you using cognitive behavioral strategies, identifying thought patterns produced by depression in your brain and working to "override" these thoughts with truth. Secular resources, read with a critical but open eye, can also be of help. Dr. David Burns wrote one such book, *The Feeling Good Handbook* (1999), that will walk you through specific strategies for changing your thinking and behavior. Applying biblical principles to these strategies helps as well, as you consider not just a "positive" thought but a true, spiritually real thought to counter the barrage of negative thoughts depression can bring.

Clinical depression is an illness that we must take seriously as Christians, because untreated depression has consequences. As we discussed in chapter 3 when we considered medication, untreated depression can put a person at greater risk for heart disease, diabetes, and Alzheimer's. Additionally, fatality by suicide is a serious risk for those who do not seek help for depression.

As Christians, we must not ignore the realities of disease among us. If we deny the reality of physical and mental illness, we only succeed in giving Satan a foothold as we come to the battle unprepared. We cannot effectively pray or act against something that we have chosen not to understand. How can we as Christians deny and ignore medical and scientific discovery while saying that we are truth-seekers? All truth belongs to God, and it is when we embrace the spiritual and physical realities around us that we are equipped to fight for a way out. In the kingdom of God, there is no more disease. Let us bring about that reality here and now by advocating for an end to mental illness—not by pretending it does not exist among us, but by doing all we can to understand it and fight for a cure in both the spiritual and physical realms.

7

How Can I Trust God When I Worry All the Time?

Case Example

Let's turn to Vanessa's daughter, Kate (refer back to the case example from the previous chapter for more on Vanessa's story). Kate suffered from some depressive issues, as Vanessa did. But they had something else in common—anxiety. These two problems often occur together. As we think about Kate, we'll focus on her anxiety, even though she has two distinct but connected mental health diagnoses.

Kate was an intelligent young woman who was married with no children. She had very little idea about what she wanted to do with her life. Although she was very concerned about many social issues in the world, she didn't know what her contribution should be. She was good at mathematics, and even though she was introverted, she didn't want to work alone all the time. Kate also wasn't very driven or ambitious—she had a more laid-back attitude toward life and valued fun and silliness. During college, she had enjoyed investing in her friends and was highly involved in her college's Christian fellowship group—indeed, these things occupied the bulk of her time, studies taking a distant second place.

In her twenties, Kate found that her life began to be ruled more and more by fear and worry. Even though she had majored in psychology, she did not realize that she had a diagnosable disorder (she had focused more on "normal" than "abnormal" specializations). Kate assumed that everyone was afraid of things and worried about things the way that she did. After a time, however, when Kate sought out counseling for her depression and was asked to fill out psychological questionnaires, she discovered that she also had Generalized Anxiety Disorder (GAD). A simple definition of GAD is "when a person worries excessively about a variety of everyday problems for at least 6 months." Though Kate was right that everyone worries about something, it turned out that she was anxious and frightened to a degree that most people are not.

Kate's irrational fears came out in simple, everyday ways. For instance, Kate struggled with intense anxiety if she ever wanted to take a shower when home alone. Naturally all the doors were locked, including the bedroom and bathroom doors. But still, since the sound of the water falling made it difficult to hear anything else, Kate would poke her head out every minute or two to listen for intruders. Any moment, she was sure (although she lived in a low-crime area) someone could break into the house, rape and murder her. These thoughts were present even when she knew her husband would be home within a matter of a few minutes.

These intense fears dated back to Kate's childhood, as she found herself imagining an intruder entering the home and coming upon her bedroom door, located first on the hallway. She also had feared being kidnapped and harmed when standing alone at her rather isolated school bus stop. She also refused to ride a bike for four years after her first try at age 5—she was too afraid she'd fall again. Although Kate had experienced a worsening of her symptoms as she entered adulthood, she could now see early warning signs as she reflected back on these childhood memories.

Another example of Kate's symptoms of GAD occurred in the car, where she would picture an accident happening every few minutes. These thoughts were present even before she'd been in an *actual* car accident. Crashes were at the edges of her mind if she flew in an airplane—and after 9/11, the idea of violent hijackings made her fears when flying much worse. After a while, Kate simply drove as little as possible and avoided long-distance travel.

In addition to travelling fears, Kate had numerous other fears that plagued her daily. She had a particular phobia of snakes, and sometimes (especially at night), when she went to the bathroom, she was sure that a snake would pop out of the toilet at any minute. Kate feared for her family members as well. For example, when she read an article about the rare occasions on which children die because they are inadvertently left in hot cars by completely loving parents, she immediately made car magnets and a keychain for her sister, who had a baby, to remind her to double check the car. She even once had a dream in which she had *too many cute kittens to take care of!* You name it, Kate could find a way to be anxious about it.

Kate's expectations and thoughts about her future were often bleak as well. When Kate thought about her old age, she was sure that she would be alone in some miserable nursing home with inadequate care. As a child, she hadn't thought about old age yet, but back then, she was afraid that when she reached adulthood, she would become homeless—even though she was the top student in school.

On top of these fears that occurred when she was alone, Kate was also somewhat anxious socially. She thought that when she couldn't hear what people were saying, it was probably something negative about her. When people seemed to like her, she often assumed they were "just being nice" and probably didn't really enjoy spending time with her that much. And Kate was also constantly afraid that she would say something wrong and upset someone else without intending to or even knowing she had done so. She was afraid that if she turned down an invitation to some social activity, people would be hurt and think she didn't like them.

Kate gradually eliminated more and more activities out of her life as they felt too scary or overwhelming. She wouldn't drive into anything remotely approaching a city. She wouldn't try anything that might be the slightest bit difficult or unpleasant. Kate restricted her work life because she was afraid of being trapped in a situation that she felt she couldn't handle, fearing that the struggles she'd begun having with insomnia would continue and cause her to be late for work.

Kate had been a Christian all her life—her earliest memory was of "asking Jesus into her heart"—yet her struggles sometimes impacted her spiritual life. When she thought about trusting God, she thought, "That's all very well, I trust Him with my eternal salvation, but He never said I could trust him not to let bad things happen to me. He *does* let bad things happen to His people, all the time!" She didn't think God cared very much about what she might suffer, if only that suffering would make her more Christ-like. And she struggled to believe the "He won't give you more than you can handle" line. Her motto was, "The safe side is my favorite side."

Counselor's Response

Anxiety disorders, including panic, phobias, or Generalized Anxiety Disorder are mental disorders with clearly manifested physical symptoms. Rapid heart rate, shortness of breath, sweating palms, or a feeling of a heavy weight on one's chest are all symptoms of a panic attack. Someone with a phobia may also experience these symptoms when facing their object of fear, most commonly snakes, closed spaces, airplanes, public speaking, and blood/needles. There are many other phobias as well, and perhaps the most severe is agoraphobia, in which a person has these physical anxiety symptoms when leaving their home. As a result, these sufferers ultimately isolate and remain inside their homes at all times.

Kate's story focuses specifically on Generalized Anxiety Disorder, which manifests as an extreme form of fear and worry. These anxious feelings tend to create avoidance of situations or stimuli that cause the anxiety. It is important to note that this disorder is far beyond the normal, everyday worry that we all must seek to surrender in our Christian walk. Those with GAD have dysfunction occurring in their brains that is largely out of their control without treatment.

In Kate's experience, she began a process of change after a particularly jarring incident in which she had to directly face one of her fears to help a person for whom she cared deeply. Caring about someone more than herself caused her to overcome her fear in that instance. Kate described her realization in that moment: she was on the road to having as limited and restricted a life as her mother. Kate decided that she just did not want that—she was going to change.

In order to make this change happen, though, more than just a sudden new mindset was needed. She found that a combination of medication, counseling, *and* her will were all required to address her anxiety. Because of the brain dysfunction occurring in GAD and other anxiety disorders, "just having more faith" is not sufficient to remove symptoms. For someone like Kate, part of what faith means is to take those actions towards getting help that will then allow the sufferer to have less anxiety and more rest and trust in God. Psychological help is part of the method that is needed to "take every thought captive" for Christ.

For many with anxiety disorders, stabilization on medication targeting the interconnected depression and anxiety symptoms enables them to counter fears with a focus on real statistics. Kate, for instance, began to be able to appreciate the fact that some of the things she feared were very unlikely to happen to her, and she used that fact to help her cope with her anxiety. She had known these facts all along—the knowledge just didn't help her until she sought medication and counseling.

Christians who suffer from anxiety disorders may also find that with treatment that are able to surrender more of their worries over to God. There is often a sense of release once the brain is treated with medication and counseling, as the intensity of the worries and fears are decreased. Trust, faith, and surrender all become possibilities as the brain is brought into a more manageable and controllable state. In Kate's experience, she started to become somewhat more open to the idea that God would sometimes teach her through suffering—but not *all* the time—and that she might actually be able to accept that fact. As she improved, Kate was able to discontinue the medication over time and with the oversight of her doctor.

Kate and those like her might never be completely anxiety-free, but they can continue to use the tools of medicine, psychology, and faith to strive at maintaining a more even-keel emotional life. Counseling, medication, books on anxiety, prayer, and mental repetition of important biblical truths all play important roles for those with anxiety each and every day.

8

Schizophrenia: Didn't Jesus Just Call It Demon Possession?

Case Example

No, he did not have multiple personalities. No, he was not demon-possessed. Tim suffered from schizophrenia, and without medication his symptoms were deeply concerning to his family and friends. Sure, Tim had always been a little "quirky," but in his 20's his behavior started to be more than just a little off.

It all started with the television. Of course, looking back Tim's mother knew his illness did not suddenly begin one day. But that day in July when the television had "messages" for Tim is when she really started to worry. Tim had become increasingly isolated. He had been taking some college classes and was really quite brilliant, but the stress took a toll and he had decided to take the summer off. Tim had been in his room most of the week when his mother came in with a sandwich. Tim was staring at the television, which was not turned on, and was startled at his mother's entry into the room. "Shhhh!" he hushed to her. Confused, she tried pressing further until she was hushed again. "I'm listening, shhhh…" Tim said as he moved closer to the silent television and stared intently.

When she left the room, Tim's mom was worried and did not know what to think. She called her husband and they decided to keep a closer eye on Tim. When he did join them for dinner, he looked detached, like he was constantly thinking about something else. He hardly smiled, but he didn't seem sad either. His face just seemed unaffected by anything.

Tim's parents had raised him in the church and they and Tim remained very active in their Christian faith. Tim had always loved reading his Bible, and that summer he seemed to become almost obsessed with it. Tim's mother always liked to underline or highlight special verses in the Bible, but almost all of Tim's Bible was now underlined with writing filling nearly every square inch of margin space. When Tim shared at his Bible study group, his points seemed to make some sense, yet at the same time they made no sense at all. His friends couldn't quite put their finger on it, but Tim was making connections and interpretations that seemed extreme at times and a little "out there."

As the weather turned colder and summer changed over to fall, Tim's parents decided that they needed to find a way to help him. They talked with their pastor, asking if perhaps somehow Tim had become possessed. The pastor met with Tim, who shared that he believed God had been speaking to him through his television, and that he could hear best when the TV was off. Tim told the pastor that Jesus had told him directly that he was coming back to earth in 657 days and he had appointed Tim to be his ambassador. Tim began talking about the early church, and how truly faithful disciples were martyred for their faith. He believed that he would soon be martyred, and he was waiting for further instructions.

Tim handed the pastor a document he had written that recorded the messages he had heard. 10 hand-written pages, front and back, were filled with almost no white space left on the page. Tim's pastor believed that demon possession was real, but he also believed that Tim was not demon possessed. In the biblical examples of demon possession, there are no indications that demons would join with Christ or express that they were on a mission for Him. Tim's thinking was not right, but he was still seeking God even though his efforts were misguided.

Tim's pastor and parents connected with a local mental health agency to ask about their services. They arranged for a mental health evaluator to come to the house meet with Tim. Initially, Tim was reluctant to talk to the evaluator, stating that he didn't have time to interrupt his spiritual work. Tim's mother convinced him to share about his work with the evaluator, and suggested that he not leave out a single detail. Tim agreed (though it took some convincing to get him to sign the paperwork), and by the end of the hour the evaluator was confident that Tim was suffering from schizophrenia.

Getting Tim to open up to idea of mental health services was no small feat. Fortunately, the evaluator had been able to meet with Tim in his own home and had been sensitive to carefully listen to and affirm him despite his clouded thinking. A caseworker was assigned by the agency, but these services were voluntary and

Tim would often refuse to meet. To see a doctor, Tim would have to go into the agency, something he was totally unwilling to do.

As winter came, Tim began spending more time out of the house, and one night did not come home. Tim's parents were extremely worried, and they drove around their town for hours searching for him. When he was still not home by morning, they called the police. A description of Tim went out and he was finally found that afternoon in the middle of the nearby woods, trying to start a fire by rubbing two sticks together. His hands were purple from the cold and the skin was rubbing thin to open sores from hours of trying to get the fire started. Tim resisted the police, and when his parents arrived on the scene he was being handcuffed. In the hardest moment of their lives, Tim's parents worked with the police and the mental health agency to have him committed to a psychiatric hospital.

Doctors and psychiatric nurses tried to work with Tim to help him understand that his mind was playing tricks on him and he needed medication. His parents pleaded with him to listen but he refused and was increasingly agitated. Finally, Tim had to be restrained as he lashed out at one of the nurses and he was given an injection of Haldol. Tim slept for a few hours and was calm when he awoke. He was still groggy but he agreed to take the next dose offered to him in pill form. After a few days, Tim visited with his parents and seemed to have a better understanding of where he was and why he was there. He agreed to remain in the hospital for a longer, voluntary stay.

Today Tim remains on daily medication for his psychotic symptoms. He remains active in the church and his thinking has stabilized. He still sees his caseworker from the mental health agency (they laugh now about the early stages of their working relationship) and he goes in to see his psychiatrist once a month. Tim still lives at home but he has started up his college classes again, just two classes at a time. There are many days he feels good and would like to stop taking his medication. His caseworker and his parents help remind him of the symptoms he experienced before and the hospitalization that could happen again if he were to de-stabilize. Tim continues to seek to trust God and is thinking about ways he can help reach others in the church who suffer too.

Counselor's Response

There is a lot of misunderstanding about schizophrenia. In part, this is from incorrect characterizations in books and the media. Most people are confused about the difference between someone with multiple personalities (formally called Dissociative Identity Disorder) and someone with schizophrenia. Classic symptoms of schizophrenia include delusions (belief in an untrue reality that others do not share), visual or auditory hallucinations (seeing or hearing things that others do not), flat mood and affect (non-expressive, sometimes staring eyes), and confused speech and/or disorganized thought patterns. Sometimes speech and thought patterns are referred to as "tangential"—going off on so many tangents that it is almost difficult to follow the conversation or train of thought of the person with schizophrenia. Certain types of schizophrenia involve catatonic states in which the person is almost completely non-responsive but awake, or paranoia (often with a focus on the government or religion).

In Christian circles, notions of multiple personalities (again, an incorrect understanding of schizophrenia) or religious delusions can raise questions about demon possession. The story in several of the Gospels about Jesus' confrontation with demons who named themselves "Legion" and stated, "...for we are many..." could seem like what we today would call a mental illness.

There are several things wrong with this comparison. First, when a person with Dissociative Identity Disorder exhibits multiple personalities, they do not appear at the same time, nor is one personality usually aware of the other. This disorder, unlike schizophrenia, is typically derived from a severely traumatic past in which a person had to retreat deep within themselves in order to escape their horrifying reality. This disorder is very rare.

Schizophrenia is also rare (1.1% of the general population according to the National Institute for Mental Health), but is more common than multiple personalities. Many homeless and/or chronically mentally ill people have schizophrenia, so if you live in an urban area you will probably meet someone suffering with this disorder. When stabilized on medication, people with schizophrenia can live normal lives and can go for long periods without symptoms. Unfortunately, as was evident in Tim's story, it can often be difficult to convince an untreated person with schizophrenia to begin taking medication or to continue taking it after they feel better.

Dr. Steven Waterhouse, pastor of Westcliff Bible Church in Amarillo, Texas, shares the story of his brother's battle with schizophrenia in his book *Strength For His People* (2002, Westcliff Press). In addition to sharing his personal story of living with a family member who has severe mental illness, Waterhouse offers six practical suggestions for Christians and church leaders who wonder if the symptoms presented to them are a sign of demonic possession or of schizophrenia or other mental illness.

First, Waterhouse notes that a person's stance on religious matters can be widely different in presentation between those who are possessed and those who are mentally ill. Those who have demons inside them do not want anything to do with Jesus, whereas in a psychotic individual there is often an attraction to religion. Another distinguishing feature is that in noted cases of demonic possession in the Bible, demons seem to speak rationally, as opposed to the classic symptom of irrational and tangential speech seen in schizophrenia.

Waterhouse also suggests that demons seem to have knowledge of a supernatural nature that goes beyond normal human learning. In the case of schizophrenia, these individuals can only speak about things they have gained knowledge of naturally. Demons also typically carry supernatural abilities or "phenomena" which would not be present in the case of mental illness. For example, in Matthew 8:29, demons inhabiting two men begin screaming as Jesus walks by, "Why are you interfering with us, Son of God? Have you come here to torture us before God's appointed time?" (NLT). These men, living in a cemetery and so violent others could not go near them, seemed to have supernatural knowledge about Jesus and His mission on earth. A person with schizophrenia is more likely to speak in more nonsensical terms that do not line up with spiritual realities understood by other Christians or clearly described in the Bible.

Furthermore, Waterhouse writes, "Authors who have clinical experience both with demon possession and mental illness believe those who claim to be possessed are very likely not possessed" (p. 77). In biblical examples, demons have to be called upon, and those who are possessed are not boasting or announcing this fact. Sometimes, delusional symptoms of schizophrenia may cause people to claim to be possessed by a demon or an angel, which serves as evidence that these claims are probably not true.

Finally, it is important to consider Waterhouse's observation about taking note of the effectiveness of treatment. Those whose symptoms respond well to medication are not likely to be possessed, and those for whom prayer does not instantly cause the demon to come out may need mental health treatment. It is wise for Christians to seek the opinions of trained Christian mental health professionals as well as those who have directly dealt with occult or demonic situations. Their knowledge and experience can guide you as you seek to understand the presentation of various symptoms.

Those who suffer from severe mental illness can have a vibrant relationship with God just like any other person. However, without treatment they are likely to have difficulty with accurate insight and their untreated symptoms will often blend into other spiritual conversations. The church must be a welcoming place to all, and those who struggle with mental illness are often marginalized in society and by the church. Having systems in place to recognize and help those who have untreated mental health issues is important for any church. This can be done by developing relationships with Christian counselors in the area as well as secular mental health agencies who often have emergency services or psychiatrists who can prescribe medications. Having a church-response plan to recognize and facilitate treatment of mental health symptoms will create a culture in which people are welcomed and treated with dignity and where all are encouraged to seek wellness in every area of their lives.

9

If the Holy Spirit Produces Self-Control, Why Do I Have ADD?

Case Example

Chaotic. Random. Out-to-lunch. These were all words friends had used to describe Eddie. From childhood, Eddie seemed like he was always in motion—high energy and rambunctious. Back then, his teachers hadn't really heard of Attention Deficit Disorder (ADD), and they just looked at Eddie as a disruptive troublemaker. He could be so sweet—"Why wouldn't he just follow directions when he was told?" they wondered.

Eddie always knew he could do better in school but no matter how hard he tried he just couldn't seem to get his act together. He also felt so ashamed when he promised to meet his friends and then completely forgot to go. They'd have forgiven him once, but eventually they just stopped asking because they couldn't rely on him. Eddie was a passionate person and cared deeply for others, but more than one romantic relationship had ended because of his chaotic ways.

A musician and artist, Eddie was incredibly creative and could spend hours writing and recording music. Though he had trouble focusing in certain settings, when he was making his music or painting he could go for hours on end. He felt as if he could simply get lost in his art and the world just faded into the background. Unfortunately, this meant that he could forget to go to bed until 5 or 6am, even when he had to get to work at 8. That alarm clock could just never seem to cooperate (if it actually was set in the first place)—many a boss had tried to work with Eddie before sadly having to let him go.

God had always been a big part of Eddie's life. As a child, Eddie would often stare out the window, look up at the sky, and imagine seeing God right there on a cloud. Prayer was always a powerful encounter and from a young age Eddie watched God's responses to his prayers. He believed that God was actively at work in the world and in his life. He loved the Bible, and from a young age he loved his church because he got to sing and jump around in their kids' program. "Why can't we jump more at school?" he wondered. "If I could learn math while jumping I think I could do it..."

Now as an adult, Eddie remained close to God. Despite all of the disappointments and problems in his life, he always knew God was leading him. The world just seemed to have different priorities, and sometimes he thought even other Christians had it backwards. "God is a God of order...." they'd say when Eddie was caught in chaos. Timeliness seemed next to cleanliness which was still right up there by godliness. He found these priorities strange. Yes, chaos was disruptive to his life. He didn't *want* it to be that way, but he couldn't seem to avoid it no matter what he tried. And certainly cleaning and organization were not his thing, but he'd rather invite people over to a messy house than not be hospitable.

As a worship leader in the church, Eddie was dynamic and Spirit-filled. Eddie's face almost seemed to glow when he was up on that stage pouring out worship to God. Sure, he was late to practice half the time, but he always knew his part and showed up ready to encounter God. He always tried not to judge, but sometimes he couldn't help but notice that one or two who were always right on time looked so flat up on stage. How could they sing about God with almost no expression on their faces?

After he was fired from his fifth job, Eddie started seeing a Christian counselor recommended by his pastor. He didn't understand why he couldn't seem to get to work consistently even when he really wanted to be there. When he worked as a salesman, he closed more deals than any of his co-workers, but he missed out on a lot of commision when he turned in his paperwork incorrectly (when he didn't lose it first!). Maybe he just didn't understand what career he should be looking for. He thought about going to back to school to broaden his options, but the semester that he tried was like a repeat of his entire childhood. He didn't think he could face the classroom again.

After a few sessions, the counselor asked Eddie if he had ever been diagnosed with ADD. Since he had never been to a counselor or evaluated in any way, he had never even thought about having a diagnosis. He thought his problems were his own laziness or chaotic personality. When the counselor read Eddie the symptoms, his jaw dropped. If someone had written a description of his problems, it would have been identical to that list.

Eddie's counselor talked with him about treatment options. She gave him a referral for a psychiatrist who specialized in testing for and treating ADD, and she continued to work with Eddie on specific time and task management strategies to help manage his symptoms. His diagnosis was confirmed through testing at the psychiatrist's office, and he was starting to see a big improvement with the combination of medication and skill development.

One of the biggest things Eddie still had to work out with his counselor was his view of himself. He had always believed he was lazy, not working up to his potential, lacking in self-control, and a chaotic mess. Years of teachers, friends, and bosses seemed to confirm these ideas. As a Christian, Eddie had always wondered how he could be so filled with the Spirit and yet seem to have little self-control. Isn't self-control a fruit of the Spirit?

Counselor's Response

Attention Deficit Disorder is both highly misunderstood and highly over-diagnosed. Because some of the symptoms can be seen in just about all of us at times, some doctors and psychiatrists have been quick to diagnose and prescribe. This practice makes life a lot harder for those who truly do have brain dysfunction in this way. However, psychological testing can help rule out those who do not have all of the symptoms of ADD and help accurately diagnose those who do.

In our case example, Eddie had to wrestle with his understanding of himself. Without proper evaluation and treatment, Eddie had lived many years being labeled (by himself and others) as lazy, chaotic, and lacking in self-control. He had adopted these words as a definition of himself, and they seemed confirmed just about every day as the symptoms of ADD played out over and over.

The Diagnostic and Statistical Manual, 5th edition (2013, commonly known as the DSM-5) provides specific lists of symptoms for mental health disorders. Doctors and counselors use the DSM-5 to diagnose mental illness. According to the DSM-5, there are three types of ADD: the inattentive type, the hyperactive type, and the combined type that includes both inattention and hyperactivity. Symptoms include problems with organizing tasks, easily losing things, distractibility, inability to remain seated/constant motion, and frequent interrupting.

In order for an adult to be diagnosed with ADD, multiple symptoms must have been present before the age of 12, and these symptoms must have been observed in multiple settings (like home *and* school). Most importantly, to truly meet the criteria for an ADD diagnosis, the symptoms must interfere with a person's quality of life and ability to function in these multiple settings. Simply losing your keys from time to time does not mean you have ADD. There must be a clear pattern across various parts of life that disrupt a person's ability to function.

As is often the case with mental illness, the symptoms and one's personality seem intertwined. Because emotions, task management, and one's approach to living are highly impacted by mental illness, it is hard not to believe that this is your identity. If you lack self-control, it must be a spiritual problem, right?

Getting the right kind of help is critical when the symptoms of a mental illness are present. If Eddie's pastor had tried to help Eddie with his problems without referring him to a professional Christian counselor, it's possible that the presence of a physical problem would have continued to go on undetected. Helping

Eddie with self-control on a strictly spiritual level would have likely made him feel like even more of a failure. This kind of approach often makes the understanding of one's identity far worse, as the physical symptoms are untreated and every effort to change is met with failure.

Medication can be an essential part (but not the only part) of treating ADD. Some medications, such as Ritalin and Adderall, are stimulants, while Strattera is not. Only a doctor can help you decide which medicine would be appropriate for your symptoms. Leading ADD experts Edward Hallowell, M.D. and John Ratey, M.D. (1994) write,

> "When medication is effective, it can help the individual focus better, sustain effort over a longer period of time, reduce anxiety and frustration, reduce irritability and mood swings, increase efficiency by enhancing concentration as well as reducing time lost in distraction, and increase impulse control" (*Driven to Distraction*. New York: Simon & Schuster. p. 237).

While it may take time to find the right medication for your symptoms, your quality of life should improve as the symptoms in your brain are targeted and decrease.

Eddie clearly had a vibrant spiritual life, with a strong connection to the Holy Spirit. While his untreated symptoms disrupted his ability to be in control, self-control is certainly not the *only* measure of the Spirit in one's life. Ultimately with appropriate treatment for his symptoms, including medication and professional Christian counseling, he saw that he was capable of self-control and focus. Pursuing wellness physically and spiritually are essential for moving forward in life. This wellness includes your brain functioning. Our true identities as children of God are most evident when we are well, as all sickness will be healed when we fully enter into God's kingdom. When we pursue health and receive proper treatment for symptoms, we move closer to a defeat of Satan who seeks to bring disease and disorder in our lives.

10

Isn't Addiction Just a Really Bad Habit?

Case Example

Melanie wishes she could stop smoking. Todd is tired of pornography consuming his mind and using up his time at work. Jose has been clean for two years after a long history of drug use. Yvonne can't seem to get off of her computer even when she knows she has a long to-do list.

These four all became Christians in the past five years, and they now attend church together. They enjoy going to their church's recovery support group, a place where they feel they can share honestly and where they feel understood. Sometimes when they have been honest with other Christians, they ended up feeling like a second-rate Christian. "I guess if I really wanted to give my all to God, I'd stop," shared Yvonne one day in group. Todd nodded, adding, "I know I just keep sinning over and over again, but I've tried everything and it doesn't seem to go away. I don't know what I'm doing wrong…"

Jose jumped in to share more of his story. "My drug use started when I was a teenager. My parents were both alcoholics, and because of them I hated the sight of alcohol. But my parents were so checked out of my life they couldn't care less who I was spending my time with. I remember feeling so angry with them that I just wanted to escape from it all. I was so tense one day my friend passed me a joint and told me I needed to relax. At first I just smoked pot occasionally but after a while I couldn't go a day without it. All that anger just kept coming back and I couldn't feel okay without getting high.

"Around 18 I started experimenting with harder drugs when my pot just wasn't enough to numb the pain anymore. For a couple of years I managed to keep a job and keep 'control' (or so I thought) of my drug use. Even though I felt better when I got high, I was miserable to be around and I lashed out at anyone close to me. I lost a lot of friends who tried to look out for me. I didn't care—my anger was too much.

"After a couple of years I lost my job and by that point I didn't care about anything. Really I was just waiting to die. I never tried to overdose, but there were days I hoped something would happen to end this nightmare of my life. I started stealing to keep up my addiction and one day I took a stupid risk and got caught.

"I spent a couple of years in jail, which I wouldn't say were 'good' except for finding Jesus. Or He found me I guess. For the first time in my life, I couldn't use drugs to numb my pain. I was desperate for anything, and one day I went to a Bible study led by a Christian volunteer. I didn't know anything about God, and I had barely even heard of Jesus. My grandmother had taken me to church a couple of times as a kid, but that was very distant in my mind.

"When I started studying the Bible, I actually had hope for the first time in my life. I had never thought it was possible for my anger to go away, but God started dealing with me and I felt a peace I hadn't known before. I kind of got on a new type of high, and actually I got carried away thinking I was on top of the world. Untouchable.

"I got out of jail and got hooked up with this church, but I also hooked up with some of my old friends. I thought I was invincible, so I thought I could hang around them and tell them all about Jesus. Let's just say it didn't quite go down how I thought, and I ended up relapsing for a couple of months. I was still praying and I knew this was not God's plan, but when I tried to stop I'd find myself going back for more.

"Finally I got real with my pastor and told him I was living a double life. I wanted to stop but I could not do it by myself. He set me up with a Christian counselor and this recovery group, and I've been sober for two years now. I don't call myself an 'addict' but I try to remember every day that I can fall at any time if I don't work on my recovery. It was tough getting rid of the old friends but I had no choice if I wanted to stay clean.

"I'm still in counseling and I go to as many meetings as I can. I'm learning how to forgive and be done with all the anger. There are days that's easier than others. Sometimes I think it would be so much easier to just use, just once. But I know there is no "just once"—I learned that the hard way. So I'm fighting daily and I'll keep going, just taking one day at a time."

Counselor's Response

Many Christians struggle with the use of the terms "addiction" or "addict." Some feel that it is an excuse, allowing sin to continue in your life by labelling yourself or becoming a victim to your own actions. Some view addiction as just a really bad habit. So how are we to understand addiction from a Christian perspective? We know that we all fall short of God's best, but aren't we just being defiant when we sin in the same way over and over again?

To begin to understand sin, bad habits, and addictions, we need to define each of these and determine how they are the same and in what ways they are different. Sin can be defined as anything we do wrong that separates us from God. A bad habit might be a sin (like gossiping or lying) or it might be simply unhealthy for us (like biting one's fingernails or watching TV right before bed). An addiction goes far beyond a habit because it engages the brain in a whole different way and harms multiple areas of your life. Dr. Lance Dodes puts it this way:

> "Habit is a more psychologically superficial phenomenon than addiction, it is not driven by deep inner issues... Habit is simply a normal process in which a

person acts automatically in situations that have been experienced before, without having to think consciously about what he or she is doing" (*The Heart of Addiction.* 2002. New York: HarperCollins Publishers. p. 105.)

Often, when a bad habit is pointed out, brought into awareness, and a desire for change is felt, one can stop with a relatively small amount of difficulty. Addictions are deeply rooted and require physical, emotional, and spiritual changes.

Addictive behaviors are sinful, but they can be different than other types of sin in that they require different and more complex steps to stop. If I sin today by judging another person or responding in anger, I can repent of these actions and tomorrow try to respond differently. For someone caught in active addiction, simply repenting and trying to act differently the next day will very seldom work. All of us are in constant war with our sinful natures and evil desires, as described in Romans 7, but addiction requires an entirely different war strategy. This is because our brains are actively involved in specific, compulsive behaviors when we are addicted, and when we are physically addicted we also need proper treatment to wean our bodies off of the addictive substance. While all sin separates us from God, not all sins can be removed from our lives in the same ways. We need more than just one category ("sin") to explain and understand our behavior.

Much research has been done to help us understand the functioning of the brain when a person is trapped in addiction. We also need to take a look at how we get trapped in the first place. All of us have brains that are designed to feel and pursue pleasure. God created us to first and foremost enjoy Him and enjoy the world He made for us. Sin in the world and in our lives (done to us or by us) creates desires for pleasure in ways that are not in line with God's will. We want to feel better, and sometimes we try to make ourselves feel better by escaping into an addictive substance or activity like technology use. It is rare to find an addicted person who experienced a wonderful childhood and a clear sense of purpose in their life prior to addiction. Typically, there is a tremendous amount of emotional pain, conscious and unconscious, that causes a person to seek an escape.

Most of the time, Christians struggling with addictions were at one point in their lives facing a lot of emotional pain that they did not know how to process. Like Jose, perhaps in childhood or adolescent years they stumbled onto an activity or substance that made them feel better and did not have enough experience or guidance to stay away from these dangers. Often, the addicted person commits his or her life to Christ and begins to try to live differently. While God can and does heal addiction instantly for some people, for most others healing comes more slowly. Simply turning one's life over to Christ does not mean the addiction will go away.

Once trapped, the way out of addiction can be difficult. This is because the brain has been altered by the substance or addictive behavior, chemically changing the processing happening in the brain. In his book, *The Addicted Brain* (2012), Michael Kuhar, Ph.D., compares an addicted brain to a seesaw. He writes,

> "Consider that someone is functioning normally and doesn't have anything to do with drugs. This normal state can be represented by the seesaw that is level or in balance and not touching the ground on either side. But when drugs are taken repeatedly, the brain is battered by changes in chemical signaling and is driven to a new state, one represented by the seesaw pushed down (by the drug) on one side... the brain compensates by pushing in the

opposite direction... Taking enough
drugs over a long enough period of time
results in an accumulation of
compensatory changes in the brain,
which is addiction" (Upper Saddle River,
NJ: FT Press. p. 61).

The brain's experience of withdrawal creates a
need for more drugs as the brain seeks to
rebalance once again.

Christians who have an addicted brain
cannot use simple willpower to stop the cycle.
Professional treatment is required to help
balance the brain through either medication or
therapy. Understanding the root of the addiction
is also critical to treatment and relapse
prevention. A professional Christian counselor
can help you explore the reasons that you
became addicted in the first place, and can help
you create strategies for quitting. Sometimes
medication can be helpful in addressing the root
issues (for example, someone with untreated
Bipolar Disorder or depression may be using
drugs to feel better but may resolve the
symptoms through appropriately prescribed
medication). Certain medications, such as Zyban
or Chantix, can also block specific receptors in
the brain to specifically help those trying to quit
smoking. Some medications designed to help

stop addiction are controversial as these medications in themselves are addictive. Talk with your doctor about whether or not medication would be appropriate for your specific situation.

Some believe, "Once an addict, always an addict." While it may be true that relapse prevention and recovery strategies need to be a permanent part of your life, it is important not to define yourself as something you once were. God certainly did not create you to be an addict, and your sense of identity should reflect what His designs are for your life. Many Christians wrestle for years with addictions, actively working to get clean and stay clean. These struggles do not define them, just as a mental illness does not define a person. But proper understanding of symptoms can help you obtain appropriate treatment and fight the battle on all fronts, physically and spiritually.

Part 3

Other Challenges:
When the Christian
Life Isn't Rosy

11

Why Do I Still Hate Myself When God Loves Me So Much?

Case Example

Abandoned. Thrown away. Left to fend for herself. This is how Isabella describes the themes of her childhood. Her older siblings always seemed better looking and more successful than Isabella ever felt. Maybe her parents favored them, or maybe it was just in her own mind. But somewhere at a young age Isabella got the clear message that she was inferior, and perhaps not even a part of the family.

After a move to a new town around second grade, Isabella struggled to make friends and her sense of being an outsider grew. Within a year or two of moving, her mother had a new baby and her older brother was seriously injured in a car accident. Trips back and forth to the hospital meant many missed school days and an even bigger gap between Isabella and any kind of social group.

The stress of life took its toll on the whole family, and Isabella's mother developed her own health problems. Unable to care for the younger children, Isabella's mother stayed in her dark bedroom for days on end, leaving Isabella to care for a baby and a toddler. By the time she was entering her teen years, Isabella couldn't take it anymore. She was doing so much to take care of everyone, yet no one seemed to acknowledge or care about her. She began acting out to get some kind of attention and ultimately ran away, hoping to find love and acceptance somewhere.

Because of her behavior problems and incidence of running away, Isabella was taken into state custody and placed in over fourteen foster homes, group homes, and girls' schools across three states. She attempted suicide several times, once nearly succeeding. These attempts and her ongoing depression meant trips in and out of psychiatric hospitals as well, and her family became less and less involved. Eventually her parents moved out of state and never returned to Isabella's life.

As an adult, Isabella has continued to struggle with depression and low self-esteem. She fears that she has already passed on some of her negative thinking to her children, but in the past few years has tried to turn her impact around as she has become a Christian and seeks to train her children in new and godly ways. But as a Christian, Isabella has struggled to fully understand and accept God's love. With the abandonment and trauma she has endured, her brain just seems to keep going back to some of those same old thoughts. When those negative thoughts come along, she now has new thoughts that only compound the problem: "If you were a real Christian you wouldn't think this way. You must be doing something wrong."

In her worst moments, when life seems challenging and she feels so alone, "negative" isn't accurate to describe Isabella's thinking. Self-loathing might paint a truer picture, as she simply hates the very skin in which she lives. Grounding herself in the truth of the Bible sometimes helps, but Isabella knows there is no quick fix. She spent years of her life living in a context where no one loved her—grasping the love of God is going to be a long process.

For so many like Isabella, even after they come to know God they still struggle to love themselves. The impact of years of rejection, trauma, and put-downs takes time to heal. On top of negative thoughts come more negative thoughts, and it seems they live in a perplexing world of contradicting beliefs. Like Isabella, they often ask themselves, "Why do I still hate myself when God loves me so much?"

Counselor's Response

I have heard many people tell me, "I just hate myself." Most professionals would label this "low self-esteem" and some may go so far as "self-loathing." I agree it's a terrible place to be emotionally. But over the years I have come to a new conclusion: you don't hate yourself. First of all, anyone who has made it into a counselor's office has already made a statement that her true desire is for help. You do not wish ill on yourself—as one might wish upon someone they truly hated—but instead you want something better.

I have never heard someone who grew up in an emotionally stable, nurturing environment with a healthy family make that bold statement. I have not met anyone who would say, "I've had a great life. People just poured encouragement out on me. I know myself well and frankly, I hate what I see." Now why is it that people in that happy circumstance does not come to the conclusion one day that they just aren't worth it? My answer: they truly know themselves. They have been told about the beauty and wonder of just being themselves.

Those who say, "I hate myself" do not know themselves at all. Most likely, they have experienced at least emotional abuse if not other forms of abuse as well. They've been told they'll never amount to anything. They have been told they are useless. They have heard all their lives about all the family "screw-ups" that they are doomed to imitate. And so they say, "I hate myself."

If you have experienced what I am describing, then your picture of "yourself" is not your actual self at all. It is a broken shell of a person, tossed aside like yesterday's garbage. The words of others, lies that resonate within your head day after day, have now come to control your identity. Abuse internalized becomes "me." And yes, you should hate that. But it is not you.

You entered this world with beauty. You entered this world with potential. You entered this world with something unique that no other person on this 7-billion-person planet has. A personality, a fingerprint, a thought process, a heart, a soul. On that first day, you were not something to hate. Even you could probably admit that. But you now sit and hate something. Perhaps you hate your life circumstances. You might hate the person you have become after others have snuffed out your flame. Maybe if you had been encouraged rather than told to conform you could have discovered that truly unique and beautiful self.

So how do you get there? Now that you've spent years thinking you hate yourself how do you start again? I have good news: there is hope. The first step is to redefine your enemy. You are not the enemy. The true, real you is under there somewhere. The enemies are the lies you've been told, the abuse you endured, the person you have pretended to be in order to find love.

Once you begin to fight the right enemies, you must set out on the journey of discovering yourself. Usually it helps to go back in your mind to the age you were when you began to lose your true self. For some, that's age three. For others, it's ten or twelve or fourteen. Think back to a moment in your life when you were truly happy just expressing yourself. When did that light inside dim? When did that beautiful, hopeful person get crushed? If you can find that age, you can discover yourself in ways that children of that age range do. Paint a picture, pick daisies in a field, climb a tree, watch a sunset, play with stickers, watch Mister Rogers. (Seriously, watching Mister Rogers and believing every word he says about you with child-like faith will boost your self-esteem like nothing else. Bring a box of tissues and just let him tell you how special you are through that TV screen).

If you can't identify a specific age that you lost yourself, just explore your interests. Take a class, try a new food, experiment with a new haircut, go on an adventure. Find a safe friend. Find the true you that's hiding underneath the self you've become. Let someone love you. Let God love you. Let you love you once and for all.

12

How Does a Christian Deal With Grief?

Case Example

Bill had a marriage most people would envy. He was married to his best friend, to whom he sometimes referred as his "#1 cheerleader in this rough and tumble world." Debra and Bill spent just shy of thirty years together, and of course the prevailing assumption was always that they would spend many more than that together. At the risk of using an overused cliché, Bill thought that the term "soul mate" would fit. Both of them were born and raised in an inner city context and just seemed to understand each other on every level.

About fifteen years into their marriage Debra and Bill began going to church, developing a relationship with Jesus Christ. They were blessed to raise two children, with whom they were intimately involved even as their children became adults, and they grew in their Christian faith together. They did their very best to live out their faith as they interacted with the world around them, sharing their time, resources, and lives with others in their city. Matthew 25:40 always stood out to Bill and Debra as a framework for their daily lives:

> "The King will reply, 'Truly I tell
> you, whatever you did for one of the least
> of these brothers and sisters of mine, you
> did for me.'" (NIV)

Debra and Bill were active in their local church, and they enjoyed and relished any ministry opportunity within their community. As they reached their middle-age years God blessed an entrepreneurial business and showered them with material blessings in addition to the spiritual blessing of love and joy they had already received. They felt as though they were truly living in victory.

Shortly thereafter, an unfortunate accident that Debra sustained required surgery, and she suddenly became physically compromised. Bill and Debra moved out of state to be nearer to their adult daughter and son-in-law. They were soon involved in their daughter's church, and they took advantage of a much-touted school system for their son to finish his high school career. Despite the physical hardships Debra was suffering, they again believed they had secured the American dream. They enjoyed a short neighborly distance from their daughter and her family, and they were looking towards an early and comfortable retirement. Bill felt that once again the only missing picturesque image was the "white picket fence." There had been many years of success around every corner, but just as things seemed victorious once again, Debra's health deteriorated swiftly and she became terminally ill. Not only was it clear that her time had come to be with the Lord, but the business that had been such a blessing to their lives was crumbling before Bill's eyes.

Within the first months of their second year in their new home Debra passed away. Bill was devastated. The pain was so acute that he felt as though he had been ripped open and the core of his very being was torn from him. Bill thought of the movie, *The Wizard of Oz*, in which Toto pulled back the curtain on the wizard to expose his hidden vulnerability. Bill uncovered a child within himself: vulnerable, hurt, frightened, unsure and alone. It was pain that was truly indescribable from any he had experienced before. His heart was broken; the love of his life was gone. There would be no more spontaneous laughing just because Debra was laughing. There would no longer be those intimate moments in a crowded room when they would share small jokes, making fun of the world around them in the security of their intimate trust with one another. No longer was Bill able to call his best friend to share victories, defeats, and revelations of the day. No more simple moments of, "Hi, I love you!" There was a period of weeks in which Bill was unable to focus on anything in his present environment. This lack of focus was an additional impediment to Bill's already difficult struggle to preserve his business and financial interests at that time.

Though he had experienced a loss in his life, Bill sensed the presence of God. His emotional pain seemed overwhelming, but he called out to the Lord to lean on Him in order to remain grounded. His hope in Christ and his faith in God enabled him to see through his own dimly lit future, as he held on to the reality that Debra was secure and at home with the Lord.

Even though his faith was strong and offered him hope, Bill's emotional shock made way for depression to set in and take precedence in his life. Early on in his grief-journey, though he was reasonable and rational in his acceptance that Debra was gone, there were fleeting times that were exceptions to that acceptance. He at times would miss her so much that his mind played tricks on him, and he would think of ways to try to communicate with Debra. Of course, those moments, as separated from reality as they were, would bring Bill back to the reality that he needed to purposefully maintain his psychological sanity. He still had the responsibility of a son in high school, two animals to care for and a grieving adult daughter, whose proximity was invaluable during this time. All of these responsibilities turned out to be crucial in keeping him grounded, allowing him to remember that he still had a life to live.

The reality of the loss of Bill's livelihood with the financial collapse of his business forced him out of his semi-retirement mode and back into to the workforce. Bill's professional degree was a boon to his job searching during a difficult economic time for the country as a whole, yet he still struggled to find work. The pain of his loss was so acute that he struggled to connect professionally. After trying and failing to find work, Bill returned to the city where he and Debra had been raised. Bill found work, but he continued to wrestle with a sense of inadequacy as he felt that he was back at the bottom of the work force ladder. The fact that his job involved serving others was a comfort, as he felt that at least he was making an effort to do something useful. Bill was initially frustrated with his new, substantially decreased economic reality as well as with having to adjust to a subordinate employee position after having freedom in running his own business for so long. After living the good life with Debra for so long, Bill wrestled to find answers for what God was trying to do in this new, unanticipated circumstance.

Debra has been gone for seven years now, and Bill feels his pain has moved from debilitating to a more moderate and manageable condition. Some days are harder than others, as particular sights and sounds around him can quickly bring him back to an intense sense of grief. Bill does his best to serve God through all of his emotions, but he has a very real understanding of suffering and loss. He knows that nothing can ever replace Debra, and certainly he cannot imagine what "moving on" would look like, though many around him seem to recommend it. Bill cannot pretend to be "fine," but in his grief he has found ways to adjust to the loss. His identity as a married man has been taken, but he is discovering a new sense of identity as a man of God who, like Christ, has experienced the pain of suffering.

Counselor's Response

It is reasonable to assume that each and every human throughout history has experienced times in life that involved the passing of a loved one or a loss of some personal significance. These experiences have caused either pain, sorrow, regret, or all of those feelings, which together may provide a summary definition of *grief*. The manifestation of grief, including the severity of feeling as well as the duration of those feelings is uniquely personal. This personalized experience of grief is what is meant by the term *bereavement*. As empathetic as one may be toward his fellow man, it is impossible to experience the emotional and psychological state that another may be in. Thus even in a Christian context it can be hard to truly understand another person's grief and process of bereavement.

Our society in general has accepted and expected the bereaved to adhere to the traditional theory put forth by a Swiss American psychiatrist, Elizabeth Kubler-Ross, in her 1969 book *On Death and Dying*. She proposed a five-step process of grieving, summarized here:

Denial—One of the first reactions in crisis or loss is denial. The person may try to shut out the reality or magnitude of the situation, and may begin to develop a false, preferable reality.

Anger—The grieving person may begin to think or verbalize statements such as, "It's not fair!" or "How can this happen to me?" They may also seek someone or something to blame.

Bargaining—This conversation-with-God stage may include ideas like, "I'll do anything for a few more years with my loved one" or "I'll give my life savings, if only..." This bargaining is an effort to regain some sense of power over a situation in which the grieving person has had to face a loss of control over circumstances.

Depression—To varying degrees of severity, a person may enter into a depression. Feelings such as ongoing sadness, loss of motivation, or even wishes for death or suicidal thoughts may define this stage of the grieving process.

Acceptance—Over time, the one who has experienced loss may begin to believe life can be okay once again, or the person may gain a sense of empowerment to fight off sadness. Some may speak out or become an advocate for others as a way to bring something positive out of a negative situation.

While these stages are incredibly well-known and were formative in the understanding of the grief process, many have noted some inaccuracies in Kubler-Ross' stages. A grieving person may or may not go through these stages in this exact order and he or she may cycle through these stages at varying rates, at times going back to a previously resolved phase. Additionally, not all people who are grieving necessarily go through every stage.

The following framework, building upon Kubler-Ross' model but adjusting based on commonly observed grief patterns in Bill's life and the stories of countless others, may be a more accurate model:

Emotional/Psychological Shock—This initial reaction to a loss involves an overwhelming realization of loss personally and then socially, being all but debilitated in thought and action except for the basics of physical survival. One may have a sense of detachment from one's own life.

Desperation for Spiritual Comfort—During or after the experience of shock, the grieving person may search for soothing, via prayer, reading the Bible or books on loss, or the comfort of others. There may be a sense of urgency as the need for comfort is immediate in order to continue to function.

Depression—As the grieving person frantically seeks comfort and struggles to find relief, depression may set in. Being aware of the reality of the loss can create an onset of depression. One may experience times of deep sorrow, regret, and incidental fleeting moments of delusion (such as "seeing" a lost loved one across a crowded room).

Acceptance with Prolonged Depression— Unlike Kubler-Ross' acceptance phase, this stage captures the ongoing nature of grief even after some acceptance has occurred. The knowledge that one must go on, a development of hope for the future, and a renewed sense of purpose is often coupled with periodic bouts of depression as the grieving person may at times succumb to sadness by a triggering sound, smell, place or conversation.

Understanding that the bereavement process is not on a linear timeline is critical for empathy. Perhaps because Kubler-Ross' model, which has pervaded our cultural views on grieving, ends with the *acceptance* stage, people believe that grieving has a defined end. Acceptance sounds a like like "moving on" or "getting over" a loss. Unfortunately, in far too many cases the grieved may hear the following:

"It is time to get past this loss."
"It's been so many years now."
"This person at work is remarried already."
"It's time to get back on the horse and ride again."

These are statements (insensitive at best) have been uttered by many, and these only serve to foster dismay and misunderstanding. The grieving person hearing statements like these often feels emotionally abandoned by friends and even loving family members. Grief and bereavement can be extremely traumatic and the bereavement can be prolonged. Because it is difficult or uncomfortable for friends or family members to sit with another's sadness or sense of loss, there can be a tendency to rush the grief process. In the American Christian subculture, prolonged sadness often does not "fit" within the paradigm of faith and hope in Christ.

What is often misunderstood among Christians is the way in which a grieving person can experience ongoing sadness and spiritual strength at the same time. Often Bible verses or passages of Scripture provide great comfort to the bereaved, yet they do not remove sadness. Keenly felt suffering unites us with Christ, as He remains real even in the midst of our grief. We do not need to remove sadness in order to "get back on track" spiritually. Sometimes, it is in the dark places that we most vividly encounter God. As is written in 2 Corinthians 12:9:

> "But he said to me, 'My grace is sufficient for you, for my power is made perfect in weakness.' Therefore I will boast all the more gladly about my weaknesses, so that Christ's power may rest on me."

As we seek to comfort the grieving, or as we walk through a bereavement journey of our own, we must not seek to do away with sadness or suffering, but rather use it to find Christ's power in our lives. Let us allow Christ's strength to carry us when we cannot carry ourselves rather than aim to pick ourselves up, forget our pain, and "move on."

13

Submission or Abuse?
Facing Domestic Violence

Case Example

Bruised. Battered. Beaten. Torn apart, literally, from limb to limb. Sometimes you fight for your life day in and day out, yet the world looks at you totally unsuspecting. Your strong façade is a mask you wear for those around you, and one day you wake up and realize that that mask was the only thing that kept you alive.

She is Jennifer. Her story is one of pain that began too many years ago to count. All she really ever wanted was a happy life... was that too much to ask? She never set out to be abused. As Jennifer recalled her experiences, she told me one day, "Strange how even when you're in it, it's

so surreal you think, 'This can't be my life.'"
Jennifer supposes that's why she kept going.
Somehow in her head her kids were better off if
she stayed. She couldn't imagine having the
strength for a custody battle, trying to dispel all
the lies he'd surely tell. The things the kids
witnessed... she shudders to think. But all she
kept thinking was, "Keep it together, keep them
together... together, together, together..." This
became her mantra. So no one ever knew she
was falling apart.

After a while, Jennifer got pretty good at
buying clothes that cover bruises. Everything
becomes about that happy face. Her alter ego...
the one who was surviving. That alter ego took
over and truly became Jennifer. The denial was
so strong that she couldn't even tell herself the
truth about what was going on. She'd get beat
and clean herself up as if it were nothing. Just
another daily routine, that's it. No big deal. Now
Jennifer thinks that if she had tried to face the
reality of her situation she might have died.
Maybe if she didn't pick herself up day after day
he would have killed her.

Unlike many others facing domestic
violence, Jennifer was fortunate to have a full-
time job. Because she could support herself, she
was able to flee to a relative's house once she
had worked through the fact that she did not

need this man. She worked with domestic violence advocate and counselor who helped her realize the importance of keeping herself and her children safe. Eventually, with their help, she was able to arrange for safety and ultimately press charges.

Jennifer is in a whole new life stage now: her children are grown and her abuser is far away. She wishes she could say that she's gotten that happy life she always wanted, but with reality crashing down around her sometimes she strains to see any light through her dark tunnel. Her alter ego kept her alive, but twenty years is a long time to sustain a fantasy about who you are. She still lives in fear, knowing that her abuser just might come back to find her. Her kids... well you can imagine that their adult lives aren't necessarily well-adjusted.

Reality. Jennifer ran from it for so long and she knows why. She almost wishes she could do it again. But her body just won't let her. Her mind won't let her. And truly she knows that if she wants to heal she can't keep walking on a broken leg. Her time for treatment has come, and as much as she wants to scream, "Just cut it off! End this pain!" she can't. It is her time to heal. Strange how much healing hurts.

She's not sure if she was falling apart more before or after she started facing her pain.

The beginning of recovery is no bed of roses. Sometimes Jennifer wonders when her day will come when she looks out my window, breathes some fresh air, and thinks, "Wow, life is good." But she is beginning to believe that that moment is possible for the real Jennifer. Not the alter ego, but actual Jennifer. The idea that she won't have to pretend anymore, she can be free from the lies and denial... that is why she gets up in the morning now.

This time in Jennifer's life is one of self-discovery. It's scary to try to look for a self you lost decades ago and hope there are enough pieces there to patch together an identity. But she tries to be in tune with the present... the smells, the sounds, the tastes, the colors around her. She is no longer trying to escape. Her past is part of her and she doesn't need to pretend it isn't there. But there's a whole world out there for her that she hasn't had time to discover yet. So she's exploring what she likes and what she doesn't like. She's trying things (turns out she is quite a chef, but she and a paintbrush will probably never work). She's making friends with people who accept her no matter what.

Jennifer doesn't have to pretend to be strong. That's the place of acceptance she's come to now. Falling apart is no longer her greatest fear. Living life as someone she's not, lying to those closest to her, creating a false world to live in... now these are her fears. She's learned that there's the kind of coping that builds prison bars around you and there's coping that sets you free. She's not all the way there yet; she still has some big changes ahead of her in her life. But starting over again means wiping away all she has clung to. She can't keep her life the same and expect change at the same time. Jennifer knows these changes will mean loss for her. An acknowledgement that she can't start over and rewind. Letting go means starting from today, accepting what she can't change, taking ownership of what she can.

All those years she pretended to be strong, yet Jennifer is now discovering a new kind of strength. Real strength, not just a happy face. Lots of days there is no smile. But the determination to survive that she always carried with her is now an inner strength. Knowing she can do this. Believing God put her on this earth for more than to be somebody's rag doll. Fixing her eyes on that day when she can say, "I love me."

Counselor's Response

Throughout its history, the church has struggled to respond adequately to issues of abuse and domestic violence. Many battered women share stories in print and online about their experiences being told by church leaders or pastors to remain with their abusive husbands. The Bible has certainly been twisted and misused by many who have defended or even enabled an abusive man's actions by advocating for "submission" by the wife.

Dr. Catherine Kroeger, who in her lifetime spent decades advocating for biblical gender equality, was among the founders of *Christians for Biblical Equality* as well as an organization called *Peace and Safety in the Christian Home*. She and other Christian leaders have devoted themselves to taking a stand against domestic violence and raising awareness of the problem within the church.

Despite these efforts, domestic violence is not a subject that is commonly talked about in sermons or Bible teachings. Pastors may speak privately to couples as needed, but rarely do they address it in a more public way. Unfortunately, much abuse is hidden and goes unreported, leaving women with a sense of powerlessness as they feel it is their Christian duty to remain with their husbands despite the abusive nature of the relationship.

In his article titled, "Why Pastors Struggle With Confronting Domestic Violence," John Shore of *The Huffington Post* offers some possible reasons that Christians do not hear about the issue very often. (Web 5/9/11. Retrieved 7/10/14.) Shore suggests that part of the problem may be that if you are not living in an abusive situation, it is hard to truly understand the systemic ways in which abuse festers. He also points out that abusers are very good at manipulating others, and may easily convince pastors to minimize the reality or severity of the wife's report. There are also some stereotypes about abusive families that may not be accurate, leading some pastors to doubt that their best elder, for example, could truly be considered abusive. The genuine hope and belief that Christ can restore all things can sometimes lead pastors and Christian counselors to advise an abused woman to remain with her husband and pray for change.

How should the church respond to situations of domestic violence, in light of these common reasons the issue is often mishandled or ignored? There are several practical steps pastors and fellow Christians can take as we seek to bring healing to both men and women. (It is important to keep in mind that while a smaller percentage, men are sometimes victims and wives abusers of their husbands).

First, it is critical that pastors and the overall Christian community have a consistent pattern of believing the stories of victims. As Shore mentioned in his article, it is easy for accusations to be minimized by the abuser, making it difficult to determine the veracity of the claims. It is always better to err on the side of believing someone who is typically taking quite a risk in reporting abuse. Going to the abuser for verification of the claim is a poor and potentially dangerous choice. Active listening and affirming phrases such as, "It sounds like you're feeling [blank], is that right?" or "You made a good choice in talking to someone about this" are helpful as a first response.

When there are direct injuries and/or children involved, the church must have developed systems for reporting crimes to proper authorities and assisting victims in getting out of danger. Some communities have networks of safe-houses or other agencies specifically trained in addressing issues of domestic violence, and pastors should be well-informed of the resources in their area. In the absence of these resources, the church should create systems for emergency housing offered by other members of the church or perhaps nearby churches. In partnering a few churches in a given area, there may be added safety if a victim is able to be housed in a Christian home unknown to the abuser. There is certainly a need for those with gifts of hospitality to come forward and offer their homes to be used in emergencies.

Pastors must also connect both abusers and victims with separate Christian counselors, and pastors should remain involved in this treatment by maintaining frequent contact with the counselors. Allowing Christian mental health professionals to advise and inform pastors can help them understand more objectively the true nature of what is going on as well as necessary action steps. Pastors may be too personally involved to judge when it is or is not appropriate for a couple to re-unite after an abusive situation. Christian counselors can offer a trained, objective insight into the appropriateness of reconciliation in a given situation.

Seminaries and pastors' conferences can devote more time to domestic violence training so that pastors know the red flags to watch for in their congregations. Social isolation, control of resources, and frequent demeaning or guilt-tripping are common signs of an abusive relationship. Pastors should be familiar with cycles of abuse, and should understand why victims, particularly Christian victims, tend to stay with abusers.

With added training on how to handle domestic violence, pastors may feel more comfortable publicly addressing the topic. Sermons on the role of husbands as servant-leaders or the differences between Christian submission to each other versus victimization would go a long way towards raising awareness and building a culture that does not tolerate abuse.

14

Life or Death?

When Mental Illness is Fatal

Case Example

Barbara became a Christian thirty years ago. She was a mother of three, feeling trapped in a marriage she had no business getting into in the first place. When a friend invited her to a Bible study, she thought maybe God would be a way out. She repeated something they called the "sinner's prayer" and started praying and reading her Bible. This connection with God and friends gave her hope and she desperately wanted to follow God. But the strain of her marriage felt crippling and she sank into depression.

Previously a very occasional drinker, Barbara found herself seeking any escape from her pain. Her decline was so gradual she didn't see it at the time. She pulled away from her friends, and she tried to keep praying but was met with complete silence and emptiness. After about seven horrible years, her husband left her because of her alcoholism. Her children, who were teenagers by this point, had to fend for themselves.

Barbara's depression worsened, especially in the midst of her alcoholism (itself a physical depressant). The end of her marriage was a relief on one hand, but she felt as though she had completely failed at life. Not to mention her sense of failure as a Christian—Barbara became sure that God could not possibly still love her, if He ever had in the first place.

With a sense of nothing to lose, Barbara found some pills to mix with alcohol and tried to end her life. Unsuccessful, she found herself in a psychiatric hospital. It was there that she began to get help for her depression and she also began taking steps towards sobriety. She felt better for a little while, but she had no support system as she had lost all of her friends over the past decade. Living in a rural area, Barbara found it difficult to connect with counseling, meetings, or groups.

Barbara wrestled with the idea of taking medication. It helped her in the hospital, but she didn't want to have to take a pill for the rest of her life. She began skipping days, then weeks of medication until she forgot all about it. "What is the point of all of this?" Barbara began to think. She thought about suicide again, but this time she needed a better plan. She thought cutting her wrists might work more successfully than her last attempt, so she tried this method. Watching the blood pour out of her felt like a rush—it was the best she had felt in a long time. But after a few minutes she got scared at how much blood there was and she called 9-1-1.

The next decade was a repetitive cycle of hospitalization, outpatient treatment, a gradual pulling out of treatment, mental decline, suicide attempt, and hospitalization once again. Barbara began cutting regularly, most of the time not in an effort to kill herself but as a way to feel that rush of relief. She tried to be careful, but over the years she had done some pretty significant nerve damage.

Covered in scars and coming fresh out of the hospital again, Barbara came into my office hoping for something that could finally help. By this point, she had been in and out of many therapists' offices, had been connected with every service possible including case management from the Department of Mental Health and outreach services from a local mental health agency. She came to me because she was still very connected to her Christian faith and wanted a Christian mental health perspective. She felt that she couldn't believe what non-Christians were telling her about mental illness or treatment. These answers all seemed like excuses for her sinful heart. All these years she just couldn't shake the feeling that if she could just be a better Christian she would break the cycle. Yet she felt like such a failure she had lost hope. "How can I even call myself a Christian if I don't want to live?" she asked.

For a couple of years Barbara held on to what she thought was the ultimate plan for her suicide. She refused to tell any of her treatment providers, including me, what that plan was. Apprehensively, all of us on her treatment team agreed that if Barbara could state weekly that she had no intent to act on the plan she would remain out of the hospital. However, Barbara had also been in the mental health system for so long she knew all the "right" words to say, and she had expressed that if she did become intent to kill herself she would not tell any of us. We couldn't involuntarily hospitalize her forever, which would be the only "safe" course of action, so we continued to check in, discuss safety planning, and build trust.

Finally, after a lot of therapeutic work around how to understand her mental illness as a Christian and a lot of trust building, Barbara revealed her "fool proof" plan of suicide. After years of hanging on to it like a security blanket, Barbara didn't feel like she needed it anymore. She continued to struggle with a lack of desire to live, but she had decided as a Christian to take suicide off the table. For her, dying to self daily meant choosing to live daily.

Barbara still struggles every day, but she has broken the cycle she was in by committing to wellness rather than pulling away from treatment or stopping her medication. Self-doubt can still plague her at times, but she continually chooses to accept the truth of the Bible and focus on God's grace for her. Years of striving to be a "good enough" Christian drove her into deeper depression. She knows that unless God divinely heals her, it is unlikely that her feelings will match up with what she knows and accepts is true. She feels very different from other Christians who seem to deeply *feel* peace and joy, but she works hard to stop comparing herself to them. Even though she still wishes she could die, she sustains her faith in God by focusing on her knowledge of the truth and the reality of her obedient life that is not her own to take.

Counselor's Response

As a mental health professional committed to serving the church, I have sat with many Christians who struggle with concepts of "joy" and "peace." A desire to escape or find some sense of relief overwhelms rational thought—the pain is too great to bear. Unfortunately, the church has typically been a place where those with thoughts of suicide feel out of place and misunderstood. As Barbara wondered, how can you be a Christian and at the same time want to put an end to your life?

In order to understand suicidal thinking, we must first differentiate between self-harm and suicide. Self-harm involves acts such as cutting or burning oneself. While these actions are risky and should not be taken lightly, they are typically done without the intent to die. I have heard many people including Barbara describe the relief they feel when they cut their skin—the shock of visually seeing the blood as well as the body's physical responses to the wound provoke a chemical change within the body that can act as a temporary release from anxiety or depression. Control is also a key factor in self-harm, as those who have been abused and harmed by others gain a sense of power over their own pain by causing it themselves. Often, however, this risky method of finding relief actually causes the person to be out of control, and the result is often nerve damage or other significant injury. Some who have no intent to die end up accidentally killing themselves.

Others struggling with depression, anxiety, Bipolar Disorder, schizophrenia, and other severe mental illnesses do face symptoms of suicidal thinking in which a desire to end one's own life is prominent and recurrent. It is important to note that suicidal thinking is a *symptom* of various mental illnesses. Because of our misguided belief that people "should" be able to control their emotions, it is often hard to think of an emotion or thought pattern as a physical symptom of an illness. Without proper treatment, a mental illness can be fatal. The untreated symptoms of the illness take over one's mind and can lead to death by suicide.

Christians often struggle with the idea that an action such as suicide could be a symptom of an illness rather than a conscious choice. If a person dies from cancer or complications of a physical disorder, they most likely did not *want* to die. Thus fatality of mental illness seems to some to be an excuse for bad behavior. It is difficult for anyone, Christian or not, to find the line between choosing to end your own life and having your ability to choose compromised by a mental illness.

Understanding identity is critical in wrestling with the concept of choice in suicide. Ideas about personality as well as capacity are central in defining one's identity. In my work with people who suffer from severe and persistent mental illness, I have personally seen untreated symptoms cause a person to act and think in ways that are not only abnormal compared to the rest of society but are also abnormal for the person himself. When stabilized with medications and counseling, someone who has suffered a psychotic break or deep, intense depression often cannot believe they came so close to death by suicide. In these cases, how are we to understand where the conscious, choosing person ends and the out-of-control symptoms begin?

Spiritual language plays a role as well, especially for Christians struggling with a mental illness. Ideas such as "...to die is gain" or "this world is not our home..." are often taken out of context and embedded in minds that are already searching for every possible negative pathway that could give them a way out of living. Again, this tendency towards turning everything meant to be positive into a negative thought is a clear, observable symptom of the fact that something is going wrong in the brain.

While there are these severe cases in which some slip so far into a mentally ill state that they lose their ability to choose, there are many struggling with less severe symptoms who do maintain a capacity to decide for or against suicide. This road is a painful and treacherous one, in which the suffering Christian such as Barbara must battle daily to choose life. If we as Christians are to continually surrender our lives to God, this means we cannot take our own lives back. The very act of staying alive is a visible sign of surrender, and it is an admirable act for those who struggle with wishing for death.

Proper treatment is essential for Christians who are engaging in self-harm or have suicidal thoughts. Anyone who has a specific suicide plan should immediately call 9-1-1 or go to the nearest emergency room. Others who do not have a plan or present intention to harm themselves need ongoing treatment to decrease these symptoms. For these severe symptoms, medication is almost certainly needed in addition to counseling. A psychiatrist can help fine-tune medications that can target your symptoms, and a professional Christian counselor can work with you to uncover possible root issues contributing to your desire to die.

Perhaps the most tragic aspect of suicide is that those who die by their own hands do not truly want to die. I have seen many people suffering from severe symptoms and who have had numerous hospitalizations become well again through treatment and recovery maintenance. When in this state, with a desire for suicide removed, they are able to say, "I don't really want to kill myself, even though life is hard and I sometimes wish I could escape." Certainly we must recognize the hand of Satan in this and all types of illness, as his kingdom of destruction wreaks havoc on our world. Death is his ultimate "victory," and as Christians we must recognize that the enemy we fight is not ourselves, but the one who seeks to devour. Suicide is his invention, and every step we take to prevent this tragedy is an attack on his designs.

Part 4

The Pastor's Role in Responding to Mental Illness

15

How Do I Talk To My Pastor About My Mental Health?

Across America, churches of all types of denominations and cultures meet weekly to share in the worship of God. This worship can take the form of silence, liturgy, dancing, hymns, rock bands, or corporate prayer. Sermons range from brief encouraging words to long-winded or call-and-response style speaking. We share one God, but our interactions with Him and with each other can vary widely.

The response of pastors to counseling and mental health issues varies just as widely. Some pastors might recommend a secular counselor at a local mental health clinic, others may have a relationship with a private Christian counseling practice, still others might have a professional counselor on church staff, and some might be opposed to anything that would fall in the realm of "psychology." If you have a mental illness or are beginning to notice some emotional symptoms you are concerned about, you may not be sure how your pastor is going to respond.

There are a few steps that can help as you move forward in seeking emotional and spiritual health, including mental health treatment. First, if you don't know already, get to know your pastor's stance on mental health and mental health treatment. This might best be accomplished in an informal setting, such as a church coffee hour or potluck, and you could reference this book or an article on mental health issues as a starting point for conversation. Ask about his overall experience with mental illness in your church community or inquire about his thoughts on Christians who face depression, anxiety, or other symptoms.

Another step you can take is to seek God's help as you decide how to proceed. He is aware of what is going on inside your body and your mind, and He can lead you as you decide what or how much to share with your pastor about what you are facing. He can also help guide you to the right Christian counselor or lead you as you talk with your doctor about medication. God loves you and His kingdom is founded on freedom in Christ and healing for all. As you seek physical and emotional healing, you can trust that God is walking with you on your journey.

You should also feel free to be honest with your pastor, even if you think he or she may disagree with you. Look back on your relationship history with your pastor—has he been supportive in the past? Do you trust his guidance? If so, then you probably do not need to fear that he will condemn you for being honest. If not, there may be even larger problems in your relationship that need to be addressed. Openness and honesty will help you feel like you are not hiding the fact that you need or are receiving mental health treatment. There is no need for shame in the body of Christ.

If your pastor is open but not particularly knowledgeable about mental health issues, you can offer resources to help him (or her) increase in understanding. Rick Warren held a large conference at Saddleback Church in May of 2014 on the topic of mental health and much of the conference was put on the internet for all to view. New Life Ministries is another nationally available resource, with their radio show New Life Live broadcast on Christian radio stations throughout the country along with workshops on a variety of topics. Focus on the Family and New Life Ministries both actively promote Christian counseling and keep lists of Christian counselors for those in need of referral. You can also give this book to your pastor for a Christian perspective on a variety of disorders.

Lastly, it is important to ask yourself, "What will help me grow spiritually and be physically and emotionally well?" Often, treating underlying physical problems can help you move forward spiritually as you are not held back by your symptoms. If your pastor tells you to stop taking a medication that has been prescribed by your doctor, or suggests that you end counseling but does not offer a professional Christian mental health alternative, you may want to evaluate whether or not you can move forward in that context. If your pastor told you to end your cancer treatments and focus only on prayer, you might (or should!) question the wisdom in doing so. Receiving treatment for illnesses is not in opposition to prayer, nor does seeking mental health treatment mean you do not trust God or are not praying hard enough. Dealing with sin issues in your life is critical to moving forward with God, but that may be a different part of your journey from treating mental health symptoms.

Fortunately, an increasing number of pastors are very knowledgeable about mental health issues and have experience referring people to professional counseling when needed. There is a wider acceptance in the church of the neuro-scientific evidence for brain dysfunction. Both secular and Christian sources continue to see the need for greater study and insight into the complex working of the brain, but acknowledging imperfection in the current treatment of mental health issues does not mean we must avoid it entirely. A growing number of pastors in the United States are now trained to distinguish between their skills in spiritual counseling and a professional's ability to treat specific mental health problems.

Remember, the church is a larger body than simply your congregation. It is important to get support not only from your pastor or friends, but also from wider sources, such as online support groups or blogs. *Wyn Magazine* (www.wynmag.com) offers insights on emotions and mental health and is geared towards Christian women. My blog, ChurchTherapy.com, has articles on mental health treatment in the church setting. The following is a list of a few additional resources (available as of 8/2014) for Christians wanting support or information about mental illness:

www.aacc.net
The website for the American Association of Christian Counselors, on which you can search for a counselor in your area.

www.mentalhealthgracealliance.org
This group offers materials for peer and lay-level leaders to run mental health groups and offers consultation and training for pastoral leaders.

www.christianitytoday.com
This magazine provides a variety of Christian articles, search for "mental health" on their website to find related information.

www.mindandsoul.info
This London-based ministry has links to resources and articles on mental health and the Christian life.

It is my hope that in the years and decades to come, as the church expands its acceptance and understanding of mental health disorders, that churches will increasingly become more helpful resources and even providers of mental health services. Christian professional counselors can work directly on staff at churches alongside pastors to offer wraparound care that addresses the whole person. Quality training at the highest level of the mental health profession and careful biblical understanding can prepare Christian counselors for this critical role in the kingdom of God.

16

Getting Help : Is the Church Enough?

The pastor's office is a typical place Christians may go when facing emotional problems or experiencing a crisis of faith. As we've seen throughout this book, mental illness is not always recognized immediately. Often, Christians look for answers within their church to help them through stress or pain. In the previous chapter, we discussed the variety of responses pastors might give. In this chapter, we will explore types of mental health treatments and the ways in which they can be useful for Christians in need of professional help.

Christian counseling is often a first step for those in the church looking for professional mental health treatment that aligns with their faith and worldview. Depending on your background, you might imagine a private practice setting with a Christian that is not connected to your church other than by referral. In that setting, you might talk about your problems and the counselor might listen. He or she may or may not offer feedback. Depending on the counselor's style, he or she may or may not explore your childhood. You might work with the counselor for a few months or a few years.

On the other hand, you might be more familiar with what some would call "biblical counseling," a more brief process (8-16 sessions) usually done by a pastor. This type of counseling is focused on confronting sin in love and using only the Bible to produce specific change through the Holy Spirit. Pastors trained in this approach reject most or all psychology due to its humanistic philosophies.

Words like "Christian," "therapy," "counseling," and "psychology" have all been applied to a variety of methods, ideologies, and settings. Even among those in the secular mental health world, these terms do not have one specific definition as there are many techniques and theories out there. The church you attend may have different definitions for all of these words than perhaps the church in the next town over. As a result, the kind of help Christians receive varies widely throughout the larger church.

So how do you, as a Christian suffering from mental illness or emotional pain, go about finding the help that is right for you? The first step is to know yourself. Are you more comfortable talking to someone in your church, or someone outside your church? Would you prefer speaking with a man or a woman, your pastor or a licensed therapist? Do you hope to see someone for just a few sessions, or do you feel you are going to need time to unpack all that you are feeling?

Once you know what you are most comfortable with, explore your options. If there are multiple pastors at your church and you'd like to see one of them, ask about their availability. If you prefer to see a licensed therapist, you may want to ask your pastor if there is a Christian practice nearby. If you feel your pastor is opposed to counseling that includes psychology training or may not have a referral, New Life Ministries (1-800-NEW-LIFE) and Focus on the Family maintain nationwide referral lists in the U.S. Cost is also a consideration, as most outside practices will take insurance or have a sliding scale fee while your pastor would likely see you for free. However, receiving the kind of help that is right for you is worth paying for.

It is important to note that you can and should make a few phone calls and possibly meet with two or three people before deciding who is best for you. If you want to shop around (and you are fortunate enough to have more than one choice in your area), be sure to mention this to the pastor or therapist so they understand you want to see them once before you decide. Some may only allow a phone consultation for billing reasons, or they may offer a consultation session for which you pay out-of-pocket prior to making your decision.

During a consultation, you may want to ask some of the following questions: How long have you been in practice? What types of people do you work best with? Do you offer advice and feedback or do you focus mainly on just listening? Do you pray or read from the Bible during our sessions? What is your training and view on psychology? How many sessions do you typically have with a client or parishioner? Do you focus on the specific problem I bring in the here and now, or do you explore the past? It is important to be open with the pastor or counselor about your preferences as some may use a variety of methods depending on what you need and want.

There are also some emerging alternatives within the realm of Christian counseling that increase the accessibility of services. Skype counseling is gaining momentum within the Christian counseling realm. If you are overseas, this may be an option if you have a connection with a counselor in the States. Another newly emerging model is one in which a church hires a licensed counselor to practice in and for the church. This is the model my pastor and I have built at our church and we are in the process of helping others learn about and adopt this model. For more information and thoughts on this model, you are welcome to follow me on Twitter (@ChurchTherapist) or email me at newhope@ecic.tv.

During your search for counseling or a medication evaluation, you are likely to come across an alphabet soup of degrees and professional licenses. LMHC, LPC, LICSW, LMFT, PsyD, PhD, M.D., PCP... Help! If you are starting the process of seeking help, you may find that you need even MORE help when you see so many different acronyms and degrees after professional names. You may feel confused or overwhelmed, not knowing what type of help you actually need, so how do you begin? Too often people who are feeling depressed, anxious, or grief-stricken set out to "get help" but become too stressed by the process to continue. Sadly these individuals go without help because finding the right type of help was too stressful a task.

Take heart! The right help is out there and hopefully the information in this chapter can point you in the right direction. First it is important to know that every state has their own types of licensed mental health professionals. In Massachusetts, we have Licensed Mental Health Counselors (LMHCs) and Licensed Marriage and Family Therapists (LMFTs). Other states have other versions of this, such as Licensed Professional Counselors (LPCs) and most states have Licensed Independent Clinical Social Workers (LICSWs). Regardless of the letters at the end of the name, all of these professionals have a Master's degree in a counseling-related field and will offer 50-minute counseling sessions that most likely your insurance will cover. None of these providers can prescribe any medication, but they can diagnose a wide variety of mental health disorders and will offer help with coping skills, self-care, and exploration of the issues you present.

Another type of professional often seen is a psychologist, and this person would have earned a PhD in a psychology field or a Doctorate of Psychology (PsyD). This person will be a

Licensed Psychologist and may see clients in a private practice or clinic setting. Often, a psychologist is someone who does psychological testing or works in a hospital setting and in this context will not see individual clients for more than one or two sessions. Ultimately, in a private practice or clinic setting a Licensed Psychologist performs the same service as a Master's level clinician (a 50-minute session) but because of their doctoral degree they are paid at a higher rate by insurance companies and could do psychological testing if you needed it. A Licensed Psychologist cannot prescribe medication.

If you are looking for medication treatment, there are typically two options: your primary care physician (PCP) or a psychiatrist (who also will be an M.D.). If you go to a clinic, you may see a psychiatric nurse rather than the psychiatrist himself, much like at a dentist's office when you see the hygienist rather than the actual dentist. So where should you start? How do you know if you need a psychiatrist? Usually, it is best to start with your PCP. If you are depressed, your doctor may be willing to prescribe a low dose of an antidepressant and monitor this for you. (*Beware* the doctor who writes you a prescription for an antidepressant with refills for a year and sends you on your way!) A good doctor will want to see you again in a month or so following the start of your medication. It is normal to start on a low dose and increase it gradually until you get to a therapeutic level. If your doctor does not feel comfortable prescribing an antidepressant or antianxiety medication to you, or if you need multiple medications in combination, he or she will likely give you a referral to a nearby psychiatrist. The psychiatrist will be an M.D. with a specialty in the types of medications that treat mental health issues (psychotropic medications). It is rare these days to find a psychiatrist who will do both counseling and medication management. More often, a psychiatrist will meet with you for 10-15 minutes, just like your PCP would.

Nearly every research study done on effective treatment of mental health issues has shown that it is most effective to engage in BOTH counseling and medication. If you have clinical depression, anxiety, or another mood disorder then you can see a counselor or psychologist who will help you explore and problem-solve through your issues in addition to a doctor who can prescribe you medication. If you are just starting out and you are not sure if you need medication, see a counselor first. He or she can help assess whether or not you need to speak with a doctor.

If you are overwhelmed by the idea of finding the right counselor or mental health professional, ask a friend or loved one for support, encouragement, and help. Sometimes a friend can make phone calls for you to narrow down the list (by asking if the provider takes your insurance, for example). You can also ask friends who may have been in counseling before if they have recommendations of counselors to try. Or if you are unable to enter into that process, just make an appointment with your primary care doctor. He or she can help set up services for you and perhaps streamline the process. Getting help will start you on a journey towards healing and it is likely you will feel like yourself once again. Let today be the day you take your first step.

About the Author

Kristen Kansiewicz is the founder and director of New Hope Christian Counseling, established in 2005 as a service of East Coast International Church in Lynn, MA. She graduated with a Bachelor of Arts degree in Psychology from Wheaton College (IL) and a Master of Arts in Counseling from Gordon Conwell Theological Seminary. She has established the Church Therapy Model, integrating professional counseling services into the church setting. Kristen is also a published author, regularly contributing to Wyn Magazine (www.wynmag.com) as well as *Children's Ministry Magazine* from Group Publishing.

Kristen has also published two previous books: *Getting Your Life Under Control* and *Emotional Traps*. Kristen's blog can be found at www.churchtherapy.com.